AF240867

RUGBY WORLD CUP

Kévin Veyssière

RUGBY WORLD CUP
50 Geopolitical Questions

Max Milo, Paris, 2023

www.maxmilo.com

ISBN : 978-2-31501-235-0

Introduction

From September 8 to October 28, 2023, France will host the 10th Rugby World Cup, the world's biggest oval ball event. The competition brings together 20 national teams from every continent: the fearsome *All Blacks*, the Shamrock XV, the Springboks, the XV de France, the Japanese *Braves Blossoms*, the astonishing Fiji squad and the Chilean *Condors*. The Rugby World Cup is one of the ten most watched sporting events in the world, broadcast in over 200 countries and attracting more than 800 million viewers every year.

But it took a long time for the world of rugby to open its borders. Born at the same time as soccer in England in the 19th century, rugby has not developed in the same way as its "sister sport". Today, rugby is the world's most popular sport. FIFA has 211 national federations, more than the UN and its 193 member states, and the Football World Cup is watched by over 3.5 billion television viewers. Yet it was rugby that initiated the first international match in history. It took place on March 27, 1871 between the rival nations of England and Scotland. Such was the popularity of the oval ball in the British Isles that it led to the creation of the first international tournament in 1884, the Home Nations

Championship, and the first federation in 1886, the International Rugby Football Board (IRFB).

Despite the beginnings of globalization, rugby in its early days played little outside the borders of the British Empire, with the exception of France. It was confined to duels around the V Nations Tournament and the European tours of Southern Hemisphere teams with a strong British accent, such as Australia, New Zealand and South Africa.

It wasn't until the dawn of the 1980s, between the growing popularity of TV broadcasting of sporting events and pressure from "southern" federations, that the world of rugby was transformed. Two events were to turn it upside down:

- 1987: the organization of the first-ever Rugby World Cup, bringing together 16 teams from every continent.
- 1995: the IRFB marks the end of amateurism, and rugby finally becomes a professional sport. It was also at this time that rugby went beyond its borders, with the historic context of its 3rd World Cup organized by Nelson Mandela's South Africa.

These profound changes in the world of rugby led to a significant internationalization of the sport. Until 1986, the IRFB had just 8 national member federations. This number soared after the first World Cup, giving rugby an international aura. The IRFB even changed its name to "World Rugby" in 2013. More than 9 million men and women play rugby, and 130 countries are members. This number is well below that of other international federations of team sports, such as soccer (FIFA with 211) or basketball (FIBA with 214), but the international turn taken by the oval ball is still relatively recent, compared with the history of sport. Rugby only entered the professional era almost three decades ago, and is constantly evolving. A sport clinging to its traditions, but confronted by the new challenges of the modern sports and entertainment industry.

To establish itself as a 21st century sport, rugby needs to be more international than ever before. However, rugby union remains a complex sport (in terms of rules, number of players and the need to assimilate a certain "rugby culture") that is difficult to apply to all parts of the world. As a result, rugby's "new nations" have little chance of emerging at the major international event that is the World Cup, with the rare exceptions of Argentina and, more recently, Japan.

The 8 "historic nations" are often at the forefront of this major international Oval meeting. The record of the last 9 editions, currently dominated by the 3 teams from the southern hemisphere, bears witness to this. What's more, only 26 countries have taken part in the World Rugby Cup at least once in 10 editions, compared with nearly 80 teams who have already taken part in the Football World Cup, which is admittedly older —21 editions since the first in 1930— but which tends to open its doors to an ever-increasing number of countries.

In recent years, World Rugby has accelerated the transformation of its sport to become more global:

- Fifteen-a-side rugby is opening up to new territories, outside its traditional framework, such as the organization of its World Cup in Asia (in Japan in 2019) and soon in North America (in the United States in 2031).
- Rugby is becoming more feminine, with a significant increase in the number of registered players. 30% of the world's 9 million rugby players are women, and new "rugby countries" such as China are emerging.
- Rugby managed to return to the Olympic Games in 2016 thanks to a more comprehensible, more international and more

spectacular Rugby 7s. A version of the discipline that allows small countries like Fiji to reveal themselves. Others, like the ambitious Persian Gulf countries of the United Arab Emirates, Qatar and Saudi Arabia, see it as a lever to extend their sporting empire.

So many new challenges for rugby, popular on the one hand and conservative on the other, which has long stayed out of the spotlight. Faced with these multiple challenges, this book invites rugby fans, the curious and budding geographers to explore the world of rugby in 50 questions, and understand why the oval ball is more than just a sport. Rugby is a wonderful tool for examining the historical evolution of our contemporary world, and *for* analyzing certain political, economic and social issues facing our planet. Now it's your turn to discover the world of rugby.

Kévin Veyssière

HISTORY

1.
How Did Rugby Start?

According to legend, rugby was born in 1823 thanks to William Webb Ellis. This young student, a boarder at Rugby Town School in England, was said to have taken the ball in his hand for the first time during a game of soccer and carried it into the opposition's in-goal. A plaque, affixed to the wall of the college and still visible today, sanctifies the birthplace of rugby: *"This stone commemorates the exploit of William Webb Ellis who, in defiance of the rules of soccer of his day, first took the ball in his arms and ran with it, thus creating the characteristic feature of the game of Rugby. A.D. 1823."*

The truth, however, is a little more complex. Like soccer, rugby also has an older origin, and the two sports are intimately linked. Numerous ball games have been played throughout history, from Antiquity to the 19th century. These include *apporaxis* for the Greeks, *harpastum* in the Roman Empire, *ullamaliztli* for the Aztecs and *cuju* in China. *Soule* and *folk-football* in medieval Europe are certainly the best-known examples. Practices differed from region to region, and were sometimes called by their own name, such as *knappan* in Wales, *hurling* in Cornwall and Ireland, or *ba'game* in the Scottish Borders. The aim was usually the same: to bring a ball, often by any means necessary and sometimes violent, into the opposing field, church or even village.

These different forms of the game then evolved, particularly in England. At the beginning of the 19th century, it was in the *public schools*, the private schools that trained young men from the upper classes, that these ball games, which came to be known as *soccer*, underwent particular development. The educational class of the time was banking on the values of athletic and team sports. They saw it as a means of channelling and empowering these young men, preparing them to become true *gentlemen*.

This "soccer" *was* then quite heterogeneous, depending on the school, and some began to codify the practice. This was the case at Rugby School, where Thomas Arnold, the principal, issued the first written rules for *rugby soccer in* 1846. One important distinction from other types of soccer was the possibility of carrying the ball by hand. Rugby is also the town where the oval shape of the ball was invented. It was the work of shoemaker William Gilbert, who perfected this distinctive ball in his shop on 19 High Street, to make it easier to handle in the hands of the players.

Although each public school and university developed its own soccer practice, certain forms of the game, such as "football-rugby", were exported outside these original lands in the course of the 19th century. The split was to take place gradually, with the various codification systems enacted by the schools. In 1848, Cambridge University introduced the first rules of modern soccer: the *Cambridge Rules.* These were de *facto* opposed to rugby soccer, since they authorized forward passing and prohibited the use of arms and hands to carry the ball.

Faced with the diversity of rules and regulations for these newly institutionalized ball games, a structuring process took place on October 26, 1863 in London. Eleven clubs created the first soccer federation, the Football Association (FA). The definitive separation from "football-rugby" was established, as the use of arms and hands in handling the ball was prohibited, and violent practices such as *hacking* and *tripping, as used* in rugby, were banned.

Rugby managed to structure itself a few years later, notably by shedding its excessively dangerous practices. On January 26, 1871, at London's Pall Mall Restaurant, 21 clubs founded the Rugby Football Union (RFU), the very first rugby federation. This standardization of rules enabled the game to spread more easily throughout England and the other nations of the United Kingdom, and to gain in popularity.

The two team sports experienced significant growth beyond the universities, both in the cities and in the countryside. Particularly among the working classes of northern England, in Yorkshire and Lancashire. This astonished the establishment of the time: *"Originally played by public school pupils and reserved for a select few, rugby soccer has gradually become the people's game. It is probably more popular among the proletarian classes of Manchester than any other code[1]."* The number of clubs and matches is growing throughout England, bringing in an ever-increasing stream of spectators and making rugby a sport that is no longer the preserve of bourgeois and aristocratic circles.

The working and lower classes are so taken with the game that it takes up their time (through training, travel and matches) and

---

1. Jean-Pierre BODIS, *Le rugby: De l'esprit de clocher à la Coupe du monde,* Éditions Privat, 1999, p.33

therefore money from their working hours, which fluctuate between 10 and 16 hours a day. More and more of them are therefore asking for financial compensation for this lost time, this *broken time.* The elitist authorities are holding back for fear that the "spirit" of rugby will be tarnished by this remuneration, leading to the abandonment of the noble values associated with amateurism.

The same was true of soccer. Faced with this craze and the obstinacy of regional federations, the Football Association paved the way for this remuneration on July 20, 1885, and set up a first national championship in 1888 to continue the development of the sport throughout England. The Rugby Football Union was more conservative. Despite strong demands from players in the north of England, particularly Yorkshire, a vote in 1893 confirmed this refusal. One of the RFU's leaders at the time had no hesitation in saying, *"the answer to those who advocate that the worker should receive compensation for the loss of working time due to his amusement is that, if he cannot afford the necessary leisure to play, he has only to* do *without it[2]."*

Behind this arrogant statement lies rugby's bourgeois ruling class's fear of seeing the sport lose its noble, amateur character through professionalization. And, above all, of seeing more and more clubs from lower social classes playing against teams from the upper classes. This is the main fear, that certain victories could call into question the class order, in a context of strong social protest and the birth of trade unionism.

The rebellion finally broke out on August 29, 1895, when 22 clubs from the north of England seceded from the RFU and formed the Northern Rugby Football Union (later renamed the

---

2. Jean-Pierre BODIS, *Histoire mondiale du rugby,* Éditions Privat, 1987, p.48

Rugby Football League). Gradually, a championship was created and changes were made to the rules. In 1906, for example, the number of players was reduced from 15 to 13. This marked the birth of rugby league.

The evolution of XV rugby rules over time

The rules of rugby today have not always been the same. While the aim is still to score more points than the opposition through tries and goals, the value of these actions has gradually increased over time, from 1, 3, 4 and then 5 points for a try. This is why the first international matches ended in narrow scores, like the very first Scotland-England match in 1871, when the Scots won 1-0.

Nowadays, a rugby union match pits two 15-player teams (8 forwards and 7 backs) against each other for an 80-minute match. A try (flattening the ball in the opposition's in-goal) is worth 5 points. A conversion (a kick at goal), worth a further 2 points, is then attempted to get the ball between the goalposts, over the crossbar. Penalties are awarded for fouls, such as offside or anti-game gestures, and the team on the receiving end can choose to kick the ball for touch, scrum or goal to try and score 3 extra points.

2.
HOW DID INTERNATIONAL RUGBY EMERGE THANKS TO THE BRITISH NATIONS?

The codification of common rules for rugby at the end of the 19th century led to its widespread adoption in England and throughout the British nations of the time. The British Empire was the great power of the century, stretching across several continents. At its heart, however, was the United Kingdom, made up of the *"Home Nations"*, its four constituent nations: England, Wales (since 1542), Scotland (since 1707) and the whole of Ireland (since 1801).

Scotland

Rugby is first and foremost a Scottish sport, particularly in the schools and universities of Glasgow, Edinburgh and the Scottish Borders. So much so, in fact, that it was the Scots who challenged the English to a match that was akin to the world sport's very first international. After some English-Scottish soccer matches in London, the captains of five Scottish clubs decided to issue a challenge in

Bell's Weekly on December 8, 1870: *"The general feeling among Scottish soccer players is that the real value of their soccer has not been fairly represented in recent so-called international matches. [...] For our own satisfaction, and with the object of really seeing what Scotland could do against an English team, we address a challenge to a team which would represent the whole of England for a match of twenty against twenty, and according to Rugby rules, either in Edinburgh or Glasgow, on any day of the season which would be convenient for English players. If it can be arranged, we guarantee England a warm reception and a first-class match[3]."*

The match took place on March 27, 1871, at Raeburn Place in Edinburgh. The Scottish players, already dressed in navy blue with a *thistle*, faced their English opponents, dressed in white with a *red rose*[4]. In front of a crowd of almost 4,000 spectators, the Scots won the game. The rematch took place a few months later, on February 5, 1872, at London's Kennington Oval, with an English victory. These early confrontations led to a genuine soccer clash between the two countries on November 30, 1872.

With an ever-increasing number of players and clubs, Scotland set up an organization to structure the game on its territory. The Scottish Football Union was founded in 1873, just two years after the English Football Union. These sporting duels, which made headlines in the press, also stirred up nationalist and cultural issues, and considerably increased the popularity of soccer and rugby in the British Isles.

---

3. Henri GARCIA, *La fabuleuse Histoire du rugby*, Éditions de la Martinière, 2013, p.115-116
4. For further explanations of the symbols of the various national teams, please refer to the chapters in the NATIONS section.

Ireland

The introduction of the oval ball was very different on the island of Ireland, given the British domination of the territory since the 11th century and Irish nationalism. At first, soccer and rugby were mainly played by the British military and loyalists, as well as in Protestant schools. The first club was founded at Dublin University in 1854. Rugby is thus perceived by the vast majority of the local population as a colonial import. The island had joined the United Kingdom under the Act of Union on January 1st, 1801, but the Irish national question, through the Catholic religion and Gaelic culture, was revived in the 19th century. A new wind was blowing across the island, particularly as a result of the shortcomings of the British authorities during the Great Irish Famine between 1845 and 1852.

Rugby was thus perceived as an element of British cultural domination, and was opposed to the various Gaelic sports that preserved the island's Irish culture. As a result, the Gaelic Athletic Association (GAA) was set up to continue promoting sports such as *Gaelic soccer, hurling* and *camogie,* and became a veritable political relay. Irish rugby nevertheless managed to grow in terms of players and clubs, which led to a necessary structuring of the sport, already reflecting the political complexity of the island. Two federations manage the various teams on either side of the territory:

- the Irish Football Union, founded in 1874, which brings together clubs from the Irish provinces of Leinster, Munster and parts of Ulster.
- the Northern Football Union of Ireland, founded in 1875, which covers the Belfast region.

Nevertheless, the two federations managed to forge a rapprochement. They set up an Irish team to take on England on February 15,

1875 in London, in what amounted to the Shamrock XV's first international match. The annual renewal of such a match led to the unification of the two Irish "unions" and the creation of the Irish Rugby Football Union (IRFU) in 1879.

Wales

The early days of Welsh rugby were concentrated in the south of the country, near the port cities of Llanelli, Swansea, Neath and Newport. The South Wales Football Union was founded in 1878, and spread its influence throughout the principality, particularly in the important mining areas. As rugby grew in popularity, England offered a match against a selection of Welsh players on February 19, 1881.

This first international match for the *XV du Poireau* against the English *was,* unfortunately, a real humiliation. The defeat was so severe (0-30) that 11 clubs decided to organize themselves and found the first Welsh rugby federation a few weeks later, the Welsh Rugby Football Union. Good for them, as these early foundations laid the foundations for the future golden age of Welsh rugby in the early 20th century, and the beginning of a strong link between the Welsh XV and its people, who were very attached to their cultural identity.

The Home Nations Championship

The continuity of these annual meetings between the nations of the United Kingdom gradually led to the idea of creating a real competition. In 1884, the first full tournament was organized between these four different selections: the *Home Nations Championship*. This first international rugby competition was the forerunner of the V and then the VI Nations Tournament.

In the early days, the majority of the championship was won by England, but many matches were disputed. This is particularly true of arbitration, which often favours English interests. On Ireland's initiative, a neutral body was set up to arbitrate disputes between the teams. Soon joined by Scotland and Wales, this idea took shape in Dublin in 1886 with the creation of the first international rugby organization, the International Rugby Football Board (IRFB).

England, believing itself to be under-represented in the body and to remain the sole decision-maker on the laws of the game, refused to join them. This led to the exclusion of the English for the 1888 and 1889 tournaments, before reinstatement in 1890. Barely twenty years after the birth of the first rugby federation, the four British nations managed to unite around a single organization, which would slowly and much later become a truly international structure with 130 countries, known today as "World Rugby".

3.

Australia, New Zealand, South Africa Why Has Rugby Taken Root in these Southern Hemisphere Countries?

In the 19th century, the British Empire was at the peak of its history, and was the world's leading economic, military and cultural power. Comprising dominions, colonies and other administered territories, it covered almost 26 million km2 and encompassed more than 400 million people. British influence on the world, and the imperial prestige associated with it, is thus considerable.

Numerous "agents" of the Empire spread this cultural domination to the four corners of the globe. Whether through settlers, merchants, clergymen, soldiers, professors or other foreign students who trained at glittering universities such as Oxford and Cambridge, before returning to their homelands. British sports, as a leisure and educational practice, are included in this dynamic of influence. Rugby in particular, in the southern hemisphere of imperial territory.

Australia

The country-continent of Australia seems to be the first territory in the Southern Hemisphere where rugby is played. Initially played by British sailors and soldiers in the various Australian colonies, the first club was founded at Sydney University in 1863. As the game began to spread, another sport began to compete with the oval ball: *Australian rugby*. Codified in the *Australian Rules* by Rugby School alumnus Tom Wills, the sport had a definite influence on several other Australian territories, including Victoria, South Australia and Western Australia.

British orienteering rugby thus had a limited area of influence in Australia, mainly in the east, in Queensland and New South Wales. However, it could count on the persistence of Dick and Montague Arnold (no less than the sons of the famous Thomas Arnold, principal of the School of Rugby and the first to codify the game in writing) to ensure that the rules of the game were preserved and that it could develop. The New South Wales Rugby Union was created in 1874, and the Northern Rugby Union in 1883, to administer rugby in Queensland.

The Australian national team's first match took place on June 24, 1899 in Sydney against a selection of British players (later to be known as the *British Lions*). In this baptism of fire, the Australians won the game 13-3. Before promising tours of Europe, the Wallabies' first international outings were unsuccessful, giving rise to *"a lively inferiority complex vis-à-vis the British and New Zealanders[5]"*.

---

5. Jean-Pierre BODIS, *Le rugby: De l'esprit de clocher à la Coupe du monde*, Éditions Privat, 1999, p.56

New Zealand

How can we talk about international rugby without mentioning the special case of New Zealand? The oval ball plays a fundamental role in the construction of the New Zealand identity. Before we get to that, it's important to understand that New Zealand was one of the last lands to be colonized in the 19th century, when it was inhabited by around 150,000 indigenous Maoris. In 1840, the United Kingdom declared its sovereignty over the territory with the signing of the Treaty of Waitangi with Maori chiefs. The beginning of this colonization led to major population movements, dispossessions, the arrival of new settlers and the difficult establishment of towns and villages in a vast, still wild territory.

In this fledgling nation, rugby played an important social role. After studying in England, John Monro brought rugby to New Zealand in 1868. It wasn't long before the first match took place on May 14, 1870, between the clubs of Nelson College and Nelson Town. The spread of rugby in New Zealand then owed much to the local education system and a special network of schools: the Districts High Schools. These schools were located close to isolated farming areas and small towns. Rugby will be at the heart of this efficient educational network, which covers a large part of the country. The sport will thus be an important first social link uniting the different communities on the two New Zealand islands. As early as 1873, the first matches were played between the various provinces, notably Auckland and Wellington. This led to the structuring of rugby at national level, with the creation of the New Zealand Rugby Football Union (NZRFU) in 1892.

Proportionately, rugby has also facilitated the integration of the Maoris, who surrendered after the New Zealand wars (1845-1872)

Australia, New Zealand, South Africa...

and whose lands were largely confiscated to build the new New Zealand state. Rugby resonated with this community, with similarities between the sport and their fighting, virile culture. The Maoris were thus integrated into the local teams, which contributed *de facto* to their social integration. Rugby would later become an important catalyst for the recognition of Maori rights and the cultural renaissance of this people, notably through strong symbols such as the *haka*[6].

Rugby was thus to weave its roots into the fabric of New Zealand society. According to historian Jean-Pierre Bodis, *"rugby contributed in two ways to the unification of the country: firstly, by creating a central authority in Wellington, which testified to a New Zealand identity based on social and racial groups of diverse origins; secondly, by exposing this new identity to the United Kingdom, where the victory of the first All Blacks in 1905 and 1906 reinforced the image of a society in the process of unification[7]"*.

It was the exploits of its national team that brought New Zealand international renown, even though the country was still under British rule. The legend began to take shape during a European tour in 1905 and 1906. Out of 35 matches, they won 34, with only one narrow defeat to Wales. This tour de force became even more legendary when the British press gave the New Zealand players their nickname: the All Blacks. A name which, over the decades, would become a national link and a true symbol of New Zealand on the international stage.

---

6. See the chapter on New Zealand in the NATIONS section
7. Jean-Pierre BODIS, *Histoire mondiale du rugby*, Éditions Privat, 1987

South Africa

The practice of rugby in South Africa is more complex, due to the strong political context between the British and Afrikaners, then between the white and black populations. In the 19th century, South Africa was divided between British rule with the colonies of Cape Town and Natal, the two independent republics of Transvaal and the Boer Orange State[8] and the territories of indigenous peoples, notably the Khoikhoi, Zulu, Bantu and Xhosa. The latter were gradually decimated by the other forces in place. The British expanded their colonies to the point of clashing with the interests of the Boer republics, whose territories were rich in minerals. A first conflict broke out in 1880, to the Boers' advantage. However, the British presence in the region continued to grow, and the powers that be sought ways to impose their domination.

Rugby is one of the many cultural elements used to achieve this goal. Rugby was introduced to South Africa by the Reverend Canon George Ogilvie in Cape Town in 1861. The game then spread through universities and, above all, the army. British regiments played a key role in spreading the game throughout the country, with the creation of various teams and the South African Rugby Football Union in 1889. Racial segregation was already taking place, with this federation including only white players, and another federation, the South African Coloured Rugby Football Board, specially created for "coloured people". Cecil Rodhes, Prime Minister of the Cape Colony, went even further, financing a tour of teams of British missionaries in 1891 and 1896 to cover the country

---

8. Descendants of the first Dutch-speaking settlers to reach South Africa in the 17th century

"from the colonies to the Boer republics, i*n an attempt to strengthen the influence of the Empire*[9]*"*. The Boers also gradually turned their attention to rugby, forming a first team within the Transvaal and even competing against other British teams in the Currie Cup, South Africa's oldest rugby competition.

The Second Boer War (1899-1902) left a lasting impression on the first settlers, who changed their name to *Afrikaners,* to designate their white community, which had expanded in language and culture. It was on this occasion that rugby came to the fore in South Africa. In the midst of the war, British and Afrikaner generals agreed to a ceasefire, so that a rugby match could take place on April 28, 1902 (similar to the soccer matches between the two sides in the First World War[10]). The conflict ended with a British victory and the annexation of the republics. The Afrikaners, for their part, were to become involved in colonial governing bodies, in particular rugby, which *"through its political stakes and discourse,* became *the historical cornerstone of Afrikaner culture and white elites*[11]*"*.

Rugby helped create South Africa's first national feeling. This was reflected in the performances of the national team and a triumphant European tour in 1905 and 1906, with a total of 26 matches won out of 29 played. At the end of this tour, the South African team already had its distinctive features: a green jersey with a gold collar, and a nickname, the Springboks, to refer to the animal that

---

9. Jean-Pierre AUGUSTIN, "Le rugby: une culture monde territorialisée", *Outre-Terre* n°8, 2004 : 261-73
10. Henri GARCIA, *La fabuleuse Histoire du rugby*, Éditions de la Martinière, p.123
11. Julien MIGOZZI, "Le rugby en Afrique du Sud face au défi de transformation : jeu de pouvoir, outil de développement et force symbolique", *Les Cahiers d'Outre-Mer. Revue de géographie de Bordeaux*, n° 250, 2010, p.253-74

is emblematic of South African lands, and thus stay ahead of the British press.

South Africa as a political entity was created a few years later, in 1909, with the South African Union Act, which merged the colonies of the Cape, Natal, Transvaal and the Orange Free State. This was also the beginning of the first policies of racial segregation of the black population, which led to the apartheid system. As we shall see, the Springboks were the sad ambassadors of this system, before finally participating, alongside Nelson Mandela, in the reunification of the *rainbow nation* at the 1995 World Cup[12].

---

12. See chapter 12 on the 1995 World Cup in the WORLD CUP section

4.

How Did Rugby Spread Throughout the World and Europe in its Early Days?

At the end of the 19th century, rugby was not only established in the British Empire, but also in other territories around the world, given the cultural impact and prestige of the world's leading power at the time.

North America

One of the first was North America. Rugby was already spreading in Canada, then under British rule, with the creation of the first club at the University of Montreal in 1868. The development of rugby then took place mainly through educational networks, as witnessed by the first match between Canadian and American teams in 1874 between McGill and Harvard universities. However, two local sports, *Canadian soccer* and *American soccer,* competed with rugby.

In the United States, rugby developed more rapidly in the early 1900s, partly because American soccer was perceived as too violent a sport, to such an extent that President Theodore Roosevelt threatened to ban it in 1905. Rugby remained difficult to organize in these two vast territories, in the absence of national federations. The first international match for the United States took place in 1912, with, as we shall see, two Olympic successes in 1920 and 1924, and one for Canada in 1932.

South America

British sports such as soccer and rugby are firmly rooted in Argentina. This is due to the British influence at the end of the 19th century, with major investments in public services, trade and transport networks, particularly in Buenos Aires. This explains why rugby has a long history in Argentina, with the first match between Buenos Aires FC and Rosario AC in 1886. Thirteen years later, in 1899, four clubs from the Argentine capital joined forces to form the River Plate Rugby Football Union, the forerunner of the Argentine rugby federation, and organized the first club championship that same year. A decade later, in 1910, the Argentine rugby team played its first international match. Influence remained concentrated in Argentina, although the game gradually spread to neighboring Uruguay and Chile in the 20th century.

Asia

On the Asian continent, rugby hardly took root in India, which was still under British rule. This contact sport clashed with the religious and cultural precepts of the local populations. It was mainly played by British officers, with a first match in 1871, but remained little practiced thereafter, unlike soccer, which became very popular at the beginning of the 20th century.

Rugby in Asia is essentially rooted in Japan. It testifies to the Japanese Empire's openness to foreign relations following the signing of the Harris Treaty on July 29, 1858, which put an end to more than two centuries of voluntary isolation. As a result of Japan's new foreign relations, British merchants, academics, sailors and military personnel abounded, and their influence grew. In 1866, the first rugby club was founded in Yokohama, and others were set up by foreign residents in Japanese ports such as Kobe. In 1899, at Keiō University, locals took up the sport and a match was played between two Japanese teams, on the initiative of professors Edward Bramwell Clarke and Ginnosuke Tanaka, both Cambridge University graduates. It wasn't until the 1920s that rugby began to develop in Japan, with the creation of a first federation in 1926 and the first match of its national team in 1932 against Canada.

Europe

As for Europe, rugby hardly took root outside the British Isles, unlike soccer. The first club, the Heidelberger Ruderklub, was founded in Germany in 1878 by British students from the University of Heidelberg. Other clubs were founded in Darmstadt, Frankfurt and Hanover. The sport's development was limited by the fact that rugby was not encouraged by the educational structures of the time, which preferred the athletic skills of gymnastics to the sports of a rival empire. This was not to be the case for another country, also non-British, where the oval ball was to find a formidable echo, with an astonishing foothold in the south-west of its territory: France.

5.

HOW DID RUGBY BECOME ESTABLISHED IN FRANCE, AND MORE SPECIFICALLY IN THE SOUTH-WEST?

In Europe, France will remain one of the few countries where rugby develops outside the British and Irish nations. One explanation for this is France's geographical proximity to its neighbor, which explains why rugby was first played in ports and urban centers with a strong British presence. The first French rugby clubs were founded in Le Havre in 1872 and in Paris with Racing Club de France in 1882 and Stade Français in 1883, as well as in Bordeaux, La Rochelle, Lyon, Nantes and Toulouse.

In addition to the clubs formed by British expatriates, rugby was also practiced in the university environment, as French pedagogues were greatly influenced by the educational systems of Great Britain, where sport played a central role. Although the British Empire was a rival to France, it was also, after its defeat by Prussia in 1870, an ally of circumstance with whom it was necessary to increase trade. The world's leading British power was also a role model, and British culture, and therefore British sports, were seen as elements of prestige.

Baron Pierre de Coubertin, founding father of the modern Olympic Games, was one of rugby's most fervent supporters. This strengthened his conviction that sporting virtues enabled individuals to excel and countries to work together more effectively. According to historian Jean-Pierre Augustin, *"in 1892, a decisive year for the development of sport in France, Coubertin asserted on the podium of the Union des sociétés françaises de sports athlétiques that the young man who plays rugby is better prepared than any other for the game of life. Rugby was therefore Coubertin's chosen sport, and quickly became the leading team sport in the French sports movement*[13]*".* The development of rugby in France therefore took place at the same time as that of soccer, so that the numerous rugby clubs that emerged were already structured when the round ball began to conquer Europe at the end of the 19th century. It was in 1892 that the first French Championship was created, featuring a single match between Racing Club de France and Stade Français. Refereed by Pierre de Coubertin himself.

The championship was then held annually, and was initially won by teams from Paris. However, in 1899, the Stade Bordelais created a sensation with a victory over the Stade Français. This title reflects the fact that rugby is not just the preserve of the capital, but also thrives in the south-west of France. Although there are many possible explanations, the presence of a strong British community active in Bordeaux's business circles, and the region's educational structure around a "Gironde League", are the first elements to

---

13. Jean-Pierre AUGUSTIN, "Le rugby : une culture monde territorialisée", *Outre-Terre* n°8, 2004 : 261-73

point to in order to understand this specificity. ^{Dr.} Philippe Tissié, a Republican and Protestant physician, succeeded in imposing educational precepts in the region that differed from the norm of the time. *Barette,* a local ball game similar to rugby, was one of the means used to develop this new educational approach. Although the game disappeared at the beginning of the 20th century, it gave way to rugby, having passed on a culture of passing and evasion. All these factors laid the foundations for a genuine interest in rugby in and around Bordeaux. This helps to explain the Stade Bordelais' first triumph and its domination of French rugby from 1899 to 1912, with 12 finals played and 6 titles won[14].

As Jean-Pierre Bodis explains, *"as victories come and go, so do spectator numbers. The public in the provinces became more mobilized than those in Paris, and rugby became the sport capable of rallying the crowds when it came to defending the local ethos. The ripple effect of Bordeaux's victories spread to neighboring départements, where school and university associations were in place, handing over to civilian clubs[15]".* The number of clubs grew throughout the Aquitaine region and along the Garonne, from villages to larger towns, whether in Pau (1902), Montauban (1903), Dax (1904), Bayonne (1906), Agen (1911) or Biarritz (1913), reinforcing local attachment to their rugby teams and reinforcing the expression "rugby de clocher". At the same time, rugby spread to the south of France, to Toulouse, Béziers, Perpignan and Toulon.

The appeal of rugby in France led to the creation of a full-fledged national team, whereas the French teams that had previously played

---

14. Jean-Paul CALLÈDE, *Histoire du sport en France, du stade bordelais au SBUC,* 1889-1939, MSHA, 1993
15. Jean-Pierre AUGUSTIN and Jean-Pierre BODIS, *Rugby en Aquitaine, histoire d'une rencontre,* Bordeaux, Aubéron and CRLA.

international matches were made up of players from Parisian clubs. The XV de France's first official match, on January [1,] 1906, proved to be a learning experience, as Les Bleus lost heavily 38-8 to the All Blacks, then on a European tour. International matches followed, notably against the XV of England on March 22, 1906 at the Parc des Princes. Despite an 8-35 defeat, the respectable result motivated the English to propose an annual meeting against their French counterparts. As the years went by, the Irish, Welsh and Scots would follow suit. This led to the inclusion of France in the Home Nations Championship in 1910, which became the V Nations Tournament.

Les Bleus were not, however, considered to be up to scratch, as the Scottish press of the time could attest prior to the 1910 Tournament: *"owing to the shortage of valuable three-quarters, it is good fortune for Scotland that the match against France should take place before the serious matches*[16]*"*. Considered second-rate players, the French enjoyed a brighter period after the First World War, with early victories over England and Wales. Even so, the XV de France is still looking for an international trophy to be recognized as a true land of rugby. The Olympic Games of the time, where rugby was still tolerated, could provide just that.

---

16. Jean-Pierre BODIS, *Le rugby : De l'esprit de clocher à la Coupe du monde*, Éditions Privat, 1999, p.89

6.

WHY WAS RUGBY EXCLUDED AFTER THE 1924 PARIS OLYMPICS?

At the beginning of the 20th century, rugby did not see any attempts at international structuring outside the British circle, as was the case for soccer, for example, with the creation of FIFA in 1904 by seven continental European nations. Rugby, for its part, has become less internationalized across Europe and around the world. It is still limited to certain territories of the British Empire and the rare European exception of France.

Rugby remains one of the first team sports to make its appearance at the modern Olympic Games. It owes this to Baron Pierre De Coubertin, the pioneer of the revival of the ancient Olympiads, with the creation of the International Olympic Committee (IOC) in 1894 and the introduction of the first modern Games in Athens in 1896. Thanks to the international success of this new sporting event, a second one was organized four years later, in 1900, in Paris.

Coubertin, a passionate fan of the oval ball, proposed the introduction of rugby to the French Olympic Games. For this first tournament, 3 countries were represented, not by national teams but by clubs: for France, a selection of players from the USFSA[17] , for Germany, the SC 1880 Frankfurt team, and for Great Britain, the Moseley RFC team. For this first Olympic rugby tournament, the French team won both matches on home soil, taking 1st place.

Why a British rugby team at the Olympic rugby tournaments?

In Olympic Games tournaments, and still today in rugby 7s, British nations compete under the same flag, that of the British Olympic Committee. This is not the case for competitions run by international rugby and soccer federations, where England, Scotland and Wales (and we'll look at the special case of Ireland and Northern Ireland[18]) compete under their own colors, due to the age of their respective federations.

Absent from the 1904 St. Louis Olympics in the USA, rugby reappeared at the 1908 London Olympics. Although the oval ball returned to the land of its birth, the British rugby federations did not set up any real selections, given their minor interest in this Olympic competition. In fact, it was a one-match competition, part of the Australian rugby team's first tour of Europe in 1908-1909. Funnily enough, the Australian team represented the Australasian delegation, the name given to the Olympic delegation made up of Australian and New Zealand athletes. Opposite them, Great

---

17. Union des sociétés françaises de sports athlétiques, the leading French sports federation of the time
18. See the Ireland chapter in the NATIONS section.

Britain's representative was the English county champions, RFU Cornwall. The *Wallabies* won easily 32-3, adding to their impressive run of 25 wins from 31 matches on this European tour.

After the First World War, rugby continued to feature at the Olympic Games, with the 1920 edition in Antwerp. But its Olympic tournament was a tournament in name only, as it once again brought together very few teams. This time, Great Britain didn't even send a team. The competition was therefore limited to a single match between France and the United States, which drew a crowd of over 55,000 to the Olympic Stadium. The XV de France is the clear favorite, thanks to its numerous matches against renowned teams and its regular participation in the V Nations Tournament. However, it was the American *Eagles* who surprised the French with an 8-0 victory to take the gold medal.

Revenge came 4 years later, in 1924, with a new edition of the Olympic Games in Paris. Once again, participation was limited, despite the fact that the Games now brought together more than 44 nations. Romania was the only newcomer, but it did not reshuffle the deck, as this team was swept aside by the French (61-3) and American (37-0) selections. The final was a carbon copy of the 1920 final. The only difference was that France, playing at home, wanted revenge against the USA.

The match took place in an electric atmosphere, with strong anti-American sentiment predominating. The 30,000 spectators at the Stade Olympique in Colombes were on edge, booing the American team as soon as they entered the pitch. Tensions escalated as bottles and stones were thrown onto the pitch. The Americans held their nerve to win the competition once again, 17-3. At the final whistle, however, chaos ensued. French fans invaded the pitch, forcing the French police, players and officials to protect

Why Was Rugby Excluded after the 1924 Paris Olympics?

the American players. The Olympic spirit took another blow at the medal ceremony. The U.S. anthem, *The Star-Spangled Banner,* is drowned out by the whistles of the French fans.

The violence and anti-gaming of this final will give rugby a bad name with the Olympic authorities. The IOC was also disappointed by the lack of interest in the tournament, which only attracted a maximum of three teams each time. By comparison, the lucrative Olympic soccer tournament in 1924 attracted 22 national teams, even beyond Europe, and put the spotlight on the little-known nation of Uruguay. The departure of Pierre de Coubertin from the Olympic governing bodies in 1925, the main supporter of rugby, sealed the fate of rugby, which was not included in the 1928 Amsterdam Olympics. Over the years, rugby union was excluded from the Olympic movement, until its slow reintroduction in 2016 with rugby 7s.[19]

---

19. See chapter 48 on the reintroduction of rugby, in its 7-a-side version, at the 2016 Rio Olympics.

7.

WHY WAS RUGBY AT THE HEART OF THE BOYCOTT OF THE 1976 MONTREAL OLYMPICS?

The South African rugby team is one of rugby's historic selections, taking part in the first major international tours to compete against teams from the Northern and Southern Hemispheres. However, from the 1960s onwards, the Springboks were no longer welcome, and each of their outings caused controversy. The cause: apartheid, South Africa's policy of racial segregation.

Apartheid in South Africa

This policy was gradually implemented when the National Party came to power in 1948. It was the political force that brought together the white Afrikaner and English-speaking populations, in a South African state that had already been severely affected by segregation at the beginning of its history in the 20th century. The establishment of apartheid can be explained, in part, by the historical anxiety of the Afrikaners. This white ethnic community, descendants of the first Dutch, French, German and Scandinavian settlers to reach South African territory, was obsessed by the fear of being "swallowed up" by the indigenous black peoples (who represented nearly 80% of the South African population at the beginning of the 20th century). This irrational fear led to a severe regime of racial segregation, with a system of social stratification: white citizens had the highest status, followed in descending order by Asians, blacks and black Africans.

It is estimated that between 1960 and 1983, 3.5 million black Africans were evicted from their homes and forced into special housing estates under apartheid legislation. In the face of this, the struggle was organized. The African National Congress (ANC), founded in 1912, was one of the main parties opposing the system, although it had to work in the shadows. It was banned in the early 1960s, and several of its leaders, including Nelson Mandela and Jacob Zuma, were imprisoned on the notorious Robben Island. This censorship and the hardening of the apartheid regime weakened South Africa internationally. At the time, the world was in a state of upheaval, between the emergence of new nations with decolonization and the fall of empires, and the contestation of racial segregation systems, exemplified by the civil rights movement led by Martin Luther King in the United States.

The International Political and Sporting Consequences of Apartheid

Apartheid progressively isolated South Africa from the international scene, as evidenced by its exclusion from the Commonwealth in 1961 and the call for an arms embargo by the United Nations

Security Council in 1963. The world of sport was not left out, since the South African authorities wanted to apply their system of racial segregation to their delegations of athletes. As a result, several international sports federations excluded South Africa. The IOC did the same for the 1964 Olympic Games, and definitively excluded South Africa from the Olympic movement in 1970.

Despite this strong international response, some countries continue to trade with South Africa. Particularly in the field of sport and rugby. The XV de France and the All Blacks, for example, toured South Africa several times in the 1950s. Although the oval ball has not been an Olympic sport since 1924, and does not have an international aura, this situation irritates several countries. Particularly newly independent African countries, for whom playing against the Springboks was tantamount to endorsing the apartheid regime.

This demand was increasingly voiced, both within the non-aligned movement and at the UN. In 1971, for example, the UN General Assembly passed a resolution *"calling upon all athletes to refuse to participate in any sporting activity in countries officially applying a policy of racial discrimination or apartheid in the field of sports, and inviting those national and international sports organizations which continue to organize sports meetings with South African teams to act in accordance with the present resolution".*

South African rugby is the target of this resolution. The Springboks team, because of its fame and the international matches it plays, remains an ambassador for South Africa and its apartheid policy. Since its inception, South African rugby has been divided into two distinct structures, one for whites and one for non-whites, who are excluded from the national team. Worse still, the South African authorities require other international teams playing on their soil not to field so-called "mixed" teams. This decision has

Why Was rugby at the Heart of the Boycott of the 1976 Montreal Olympics?

particularly affected the New Zealand All Blacks, whose squad is partly made up of mixed-race players of Maori origin. They were not allowed to travel to Africa for a tour of matches in 1959, a decision that provoked controversy and indignation among the New Zealand population.

The All Blacks Behind the 1976 Olympic Boycott

From the 1960s onwards, these practices were less and less tolerated by other nations, and international criticism of apartheid hardened. Small adjustments, however, enabled the Springboks *to* break out of their isolation. In 1976, for example, New Zealand planned to take part in a match tour on South African soil with a "mixed" team. But the political context once again caught up with South Africa. In June 1976, major demonstrations broke out in the Soweto district of Johannesburg, as the black population took offence at a new law requiring Afrikaans to be taught as a second language. The demands turned into riots, which were put down in bloodshed (between 300 and 600 dead).

This massacre had a strong international echo. The member countries of the Organization of African Unity (OAU) reacted, urging that all UN resolutions against the apartheid regime in South Africa be implemented. Including in sport, just a few weeks before the start of the Montreal Olympic Games. For the OAU, the All Blacks' tour of South Africa in the summer of 1976 was *de facto* tantamount to New Zealand condoning the massacres and apartheid perpetrated by the South African authorities.

The OAU thus took four decisions, specifically concerning New Zealand's presence at the Olympics: condemnation of its links with South Africa, an appeal to the IOC to prohibit the participation of the New Zealand delegation in the Games, an invitation to all OAU member states to boycott the Games if New Zealand took part, and an appeal to the international community to show solidarity with Africa[20]. These grievances were relayed by 16 African Olympic Committees to IOC President Lord Killanin, who called for New Zealand's definitive exclusion from the Olympics. If nothing is done, they will boycott the Games.

However, the IOC is trying to maintain its neutral stance and a certain "apolitical" approach to the sport. The main justification: the All Blacks are indeed taking part in a tour of South Africa in defiance of UN resolutions, but rugby is not a sport of the Olympic movement. The IOC is therefore not competent to exclude New Zealand's Olympic delegation from the Games. The response was swift. Faced with the lack of decisions, 22 African national delegations packed up and withdrew from the Olympic Games, a few hours before the start of the Opening Ceremony.

This event, in the midst of the increasingly televised sporting concert of nations, had a strong international impact, which was not without consequences. In 1977, the Commonwealth countries signed the Gleneagles Agreement, pledging to take all measures to discourage contact or competition between their nationals and sports organizations, teams or athletes from South Africa or any other racially segregated country. In the same year, the United Nations General Assembly adopts the "International Declaration against Apartheid in Sports".

---

20. Éric MONNIN and Catherine MONNIN, "Le boycott politique des Jeux olympiques de Montréal", *Relations internationales*, 2008/2 (n°134), p.93-113

The IOC was only just beginning to politicize its Olympic Games. The 1980 Moscow and 1984 Los Angeles editions were held in the political context of the Cold War era, and both the USA and its allies, and the USSR and its allies boycotted the Games. Sporting representation was increasingly becoming a crucial political issue, and the popularity of major sporting events, thanks to their television broadcasting and growing media profile, only served to reinforce this phenomenon.

8.
How Did International Rugby Develop up to 1987?

Excluded from the Olympic Games from 1924 onwards, international rugby remained confined to the V Nations Tournament and the occasional clash and tour between teams from the northern and southern hemispheres. It was during a tour of Europe in 1924 that the All Blacks acquired a new nickname, the *Invincibles*, after winning all their matches.

The V Nations Tournament also experienced some turbulence. The IRFB decided to exclude France in 1931. At issue was the French Rugby Federation's (FFR) failure to take action against "brown amateurism", i.e. the practice of paying players when the laws of rugby forbid it. The other dispute concerns the France-Wales match of April 21, 1930. Although the Tricolores lost 11-0, it was above all the brutality of the players and supporters that incensed the British authorities. In 1931, fourteen French rugby clubs seceded from the FFR for the same two reasons (opposition to player pay and violence), forming the Union française du rugby amateur (UFRA).

Deprived of tournaments and tours by southern hemisphere nations, France tried to preserve its international dimension. In 1934, it turned to other European countries to form the Fédération Internationale de Rugby Amateur (FIRA). At the time, it comprised ten countries: France, Germany, Belgium, Spain, the Netherlands, Italy, Portugal and Romania, Sweden and Catalonia[21]. Four European "tournaments" were organized between 1935 and 1938, all won by the XV de France, including the 1936 tournament in Berlin just a few months before Adolf Hitler's ill-fated 1936 Olympic Games. The sporting and popular appeal of this competition was less than that of the V Nations Tournament, but this outline of rugby's European construction paved the way for its timid internationalization.

It wasn't until after the Second World War that the IRFB reinstated France to the Tournament in 1947, and finally allowed other federations to join the governing body (New Zealand and South Africa in 1948, Australia in 1949). The development of means of transport and communication also enabled more regular meetings between teams from the northern and southern hemispheres. It also enabled selections from small Pacific archipelagos, where rugby had found a resonance with the local population and customs, to break out of their isolation, as in the case of Fiji, Tonga and Western Samoa[22]. As for the V Nations Tournament, it is developing a definite popular interest due to the renewed sporting stakes, notably due to the first tournaments won by the XV de France from 1959 onwards.

Despite the beginnings of a new globalization, and the use of the sport by new independent nations to exist in the eyes of the

---

21. After Franco's victory in the Spanish Civil War in 1939, the dictator Franco forced the Catalan federation to become part of the Spanish federation, thereby losing its status as a member.
22. For further details, please refer to the chapters in the NATIONS section.

world, the borders of rugby are struggling to open up, and the world of rugby remains confined to its traditional nations. This is due to the fact that the IRFB is still heavily influenced by rugby's *Home Nations*. The major international rugby organization of the time did not want to weaken the amateur model of rugby with a competition that could bring in a significant source of revenue. And thus pave the way for the professionalization of the sport. Sporting competitions were gaining in appeal with the start of radio and, later, television broadcasts of the Olympic Games and soccer World Cups.

In the absence of any other major international rugby structure, a few new, smaller-scale competitions were created: the South American Rugby Championship from 1951 (Argentina, Brazil, Chile, Uruguay), the Asian Rugby Championship from 1969 (Japan, Hong Kong, South Korea, Thailand, Taiwan) and, much later, in 1982, the Pacific Tri-Nations between the archipelagos of Fiji, Tonga and Western Samoa.

There are few competitions on the African continent. Many countries gained their independence as a result of the decolonization process, and rugby did not really develop there, the sport being particularly practiced by populations of European origin and seen as a legacy of colonialism. Moreover, the most visible African team at the time was South Africa, the face of apartheid's policy of racial segregation.

In Europe, embryonic nations' championships were held in 1952 and 1954. It wasn't until 1965 that FIRA proposed a real alternative with the European Nations Cup. The first edition brought together 9 teams (Italy, West Germany, Czechoslovakia, Romania, Spain, Belgium, Netherlands, Portugal and France). French rugby remains attached to this organization, but the obvious difference in level means that France sends a second team (France A), generally made up of students and its best hopefuls. Given the difference in skill levels, a special format is introduced: teams are divided into two divisions, with promotion and relegation taking place over a season of matches in 1965 and 1966. France won the first division, while Portugal won at the lower level.

Despite a much lower level of media coverage and interest than the V Nations Tournament, the European Cup is a long-standing event, which continues to be organized every season, with more and more participants. The 25th edition, in 1985, brought together 18 national teams, even beyond Europe with the presence of Morocco and Tunisia. However, the event was still marked by the clear domination of France (bis) and a podium often completed by the same teams (Romania, Italy, USSR). In 1987, the French A team won 16 of the 21 possible titles, leaving the other 5 to the Romanian XV.

However, the major rugby tournament that predominates during this period remains the Tournament, and international rugby is limited to the various tours between the nations of the northern and southern hemispheres. Australia and New Zealand, meanwhile, are keen to break out of their isolation by staging a real World Cup.

WORLD CUP

9.
WHY DID RUGBY HAVE TO WAIT UNTIL 1987 FOR ITS FIRST WORLD CUP?

At a time when more and more sporting competitions are emerging, rugby's world governing body, the IRFB, remains opposed to the idea of an international tournament. And yet, as early as 1945, several ideas were put forward to provide rugby with a world tournament worthy of the name, like other sports such as soccer and its World Cup. But nothing came of it. Despite the introduction of Southern Hemisphere nations to the IRFB's decision-making bodies in 1949, rugby's major competition in the second half of the 20th century remained the V Nations Tournament, and was therefore limited to a small part of Europe.

However, the Tournament was overtaken by the age of modernity. With the advent of television, sporting competitions became programs that could attract ratings. In 1954, the BCC began broadcasting the Tournament on television, opening rugby up to a wider audience and new sources of revenue. However, the opening up of the sport remained timid, as rugby union was still very attached to its traditions. There was a great fear that the financial resources generated by an international competition would corrupt amateurism and the essence of the sport.

For their part, the nations of the southern hemisphere are beginning to think about their future. Indeed, Australia and New Zealand, because of the distance, still have few opportunities to face other selections, apart from European tours. All the more so as the South African team has been ostracized for its apartheid policies.[23] The two giants of Oceania therefore have only the Bledisloe Cup[24] to add to their trophy cabinets. As a result, the debate within the IRFB has become increasingly pressing.

Major sporting competitions such as the Olympic Games and the Football World Cup attracted huge audiences, with millions of viewers in the early days of television broadcasting. From the 1960s onwards, several initiatives emerged from the nations of the South. For example, Harold Tolhurst and Jock Kellaher, two members of the Australian rugby federation, proposed that a world championship be held on their soil. Other projects followed, but the IRFB definitively closed the door on these attempts. In 1968, it prohibited its member countries from taking part in an international tournament modelled on the World Cup.

Nevertheless, the Australians and New Zealanders have found a strong ally in promoting this project: France. Since 1945, French rugby leaders have repeatedly proposed a larger international tournament. The situation changed in 1978 when France, which had been involved in the V Nations Tournament since 1910, (finally) joined the IRFB Board of Directors. Frenchman Albert Ferrasse

---

23. See chapter 6 in the HISTORY section
24. Since 1932, the Bledisloe Cup has been the name of the trophy won between the Australian and New Zealand XV rugby teams.

even became Chairman in 1979. He is one of the leading figures in the French Rugby Federation and, above all, a fervent supporter of the World Cup. But his decision-making power remained weak in the face of British and Irish intransigence.

At the dawn of the 1980s, attempts to organize a World Cup were once again firmly rejected by the IRFB. The IRFB was concerned about the impact it would have on historic touring schedules, the V Nations and the fact that the competition would be a new means of pressuring players to pay and professionalizing rugby. However, the sport's traditions would not survive the 1980s and the upheaval of the "small" world of rugby.

10.

Why Was the First Rugby World Cup Hosted by New Zealand and Australia?

At the dawn of the 1980s, the hegemonic structure of world rugby, the IRFB, continued to oppose the organization of a Rugby World Cup. However, the nations of the southern hemisphere raised their voices year after year and tried to convince, even seduce, their British partners. In 1979, Bill McLaughin, president of the Australian Rugby Union, proposed the creation of a World Cup in 1988 to celebrate Australia's bicentenary. Three years later, New Zealand followed suit, proposing that an international competition be held in the British Isles during the 1985-1986 season.

The following years were decisive. In 1983 and 1984, the Australian and New Zealand federations each proposed a concrete World Cup project to the IRFB. In view of the keen interest shown by these two major countries, the IRFB opened the way and launched a feasibility study into the organization of such a tournament. The IRFB Board met in Paris on March 21, 1985 and, despite the reluctance of the British and Irish federations, the principle of a Rugby

World Cup was definitively voted in. Not surprisingly, Australia and New Zealand were named co-hosts. The event is scheduled for 1987, so as not to compete with the broadcasting of the Olympic Games and the World Cup, which take place in even-numbered years.

The format of the competition was still to be worked out. In the end, 16 teams were invited, divided into 4 groups of 4, including 7 of the 8 IRFB member countries (New Zealand, Australia, England, Scotland, Ireland, Wales and France), with the exception of South Africa. The South African authorities did not wish to take part in the competition because of apartheid. The presence of the Springboks could have had a negative impact on this first World Cup, with the possibility of a boycott by certain countries.

That's what this World Cup is all about. That it goes beyond the traditional circle of rugby's historic nations. That it becomes a truly international tournament. Nine further invitations have been extended to national teams whose results have shown promise. 3 for the Americas (Canada, USA, Argentina), 2 for Oceania (Fiji, Tonga), 1 for Asia (Japan), 1 for Africa (Zimbabwe) and 2 for Europe (Italy, Romania). An invitation was also extended to the USSR, but the latter declined. The reason: South Africa. Although absent from the competition, South Africa had not been excluded from the IRFB because of its apartheid policy. The Soviets therefore refused to take part, a few years before the break-up of the USSR.

The first match in the history of the Rugby World Cup took place on May 22, 1987, between New Zealand and Italy. The lesson given by Kiwi rugby to the Azzurri XV (70-6) was only a foretaste of the competition, as the All Blacks dominated head and shoulders throughout. Elsewhere, there were few surprises. The tournament has seen a number of one-sided matches, with the level of play offered by the historic nations well above the rest. Half of the 24 games in the group phase saw a team score 40 points or more. Examples include Ireland-Canada (46-19), England-Japan (60-7) and France-Zimbabwe (70-12). The 7 IRFB teams thus came through the group stages with ease to reach the quarter-finals. In the absence of South Africa, it was the Fiji team that clinched the eighth and final ticket, after going toe-to-toe with Italy and Argentina.

The host countries reach the semi-finals. While New Zealand easily qualified for the final, after a 49-6 victory over Wales, their Australian neighbors lost to France (30-24). However, Les Bleus were no match for the All Blacks, who won the final 29-9 in front of 48,000 euphoric spectators at Auckland's Eden Park[25]. New Zealand captain David Kirk became the first player to lift the Rugby World Cup trophy: the Webb Ellis Trophy, named after the legendary "inventor of rugby".

With 300 million viewers and broadcasts to 17 countries[26], this first World Cup was a far cry from the standards of other leading televised sporting competitions of the time, such as the Olympic Games or the World Football Championship. But there's more to it than that, as it represented a new development for rugby. This competition is the first step towards enabling the world of rugby to extend to the four corners of the planet.

25. Denis LALANNE, *Nous reviendrons à Eden Park: le fabuleux roman de la Coupe du monde de rugby 1987*, éditions Calmann-Lévy, 1987
26. Steven PYE, *"We take the Rugby World Cup for granted but it nearly didn't exist"*, TheGuardian.com, September 11, 2015

11.

HOW DID THE 1991 WORLD CUP BRING ABOUT THE FIRST TRUE GLOBALIZATION OF RUGBY?

The first World Cup in 1987 brought rugby to international prominence. The ranks of the IRFB, composed of just 8 members until 1986, expanded dramatically. Between 1987 and 1990, 35 new countries joined the world rugby body, bringing the total to 43. From Europe (Germany, Romania, Italy...) to the Americas (USA, Canada, Argentina, Uruguay...), Asia (Japan, Sri Lanka, Malaysia...), Africa (Ivory Coast, Namibia, Tunisia...) and the astonishing selections from the "small" Pacific archipelagos (Fiji, Tonga, Samoa). With this new international base, the conditions are ripe for a second World Cup.

This time, the tournament takes place in the Northern Hemisphere and is organized by the V Nations Tournament countries. Playing fields include the iconic stadiums of Twickenham (England), Murrayfield (Scotland), Arms Park (Wales), Lansdowne Road (Ireland) and the Parc des Princes (France). The format, meanwhile, has changed little. 16 teams are still scheduled, with automatic qualification for the 8 national teams who reached the quarter-finals at the 1987 edition. Fiji therefore qualified, while South Africa, in the midst of its post-apartheid political transition, did not take part in the competition.

However, there has been a change in the qualification system for the remaining 8 teams. To cope with the influx of new teams, the IRFB introduced a system of qualifying rounds. 25 nations took part, including Denmark, the Netherlands, Morocco, South Korea and Israel. Despite this opening-up, the final line-up for the 1991 World Cup remained virtually unchanged. The only change from 1987 is that Western Samoa[27], following their victory over Tonga.

It was the Samoan XV who provided the first real surprise in the history of this World Cup. On their debut, they beat Wales 16-13 at Arms Park in Cardiff. The Welsh never recovered from this defeat and were eliminated from the group stages. The other surprise came from Canada, who managed to secure a ticket to the quarter-finals by finishing 2nd in their group, behind France but ahead of Romania and Fiji. This means two new nations in the quarter-final line-up. The surprises stop here, however. The Canadians, despite putting up solid resistance, lost out to the All Blacks (13-29), while Samoa were eliminated in the quarter-finals by Scotland (6-28).

The Scots, on the back of their Grand Slam victory in the 1991 V Nations Tournament, have the wind in their sails and are hoping for their first world title. The setting for the semi-final has all the ingredients needed to ensure that this future title goes down in sporting legend. The match is being played against England's arch-rivals in the home of *Scottish* rugby, Edinburgh's Murrayfield Stadium.

---

27. Western Samoa was so named from 1962, the date of its independence, until 1997, when the word "Western" was removed from Samoa

Unfortunately, the XV de la Rose defeated the XV du Chardon[28] 9-6. In the other semi-final, a southern hemisphere duel pitted Australia against New Zealand, with the Wallabies coming out on top (16-6). The title of world champion seems to be in the grasp of the English. Especially since they are playing at their historic Twickenham stadium. However, the 56,000 spectators did not witness the victory of the mother nation of rugby, and it was the Australians who defeated the English 12-6.

This world title has led to a resurgence of interest in XV rugby in Australia, which has been rivalled in popularity by XIII rugby and Australian soccer. Around 150,000 people will gather in Sydney to celebrate the victorious Wallabies after their return. Player Tim Horan declared, *"It was just incredible. I don't think we realized the power we had until we went back to Australia, showing the World Cup to schools and clubs. We didn't realize how much it was going to inspire the next young generation. It probably rekindled the love of rugby in Australia[29]."*

For this first World Cup in the northern hemisphere, the trophy remains in the hands of the southern hemisphere. Aside from the result, the World Cup has undergone an interesting evolution, whether in terms of participants (35 countries including the qualifiers), broadcasting (over 150 countries broadcast the competition), or economic spin-offs with new sponsors. Between 1991 and 1995, 15 national rugby federations joined the IRFB, bringing the total to 58. It should be noted that several newly independent European countries following the collapse of the Soviet bloc, such as Ukraine,

---

28. Please refer to the NATIONS chapters for a better understanding of the symbols of the different selections
29. Sam WORTHINGTON, "Wallabies 1991 Rugby World Cup heroes reflect on that glory 30 years on", wwos.nine.com, Nov. 5, 2021

How Did the 1991 World Cup Bring about the First True Globalization of Rugby?

Georgia and Latvia, joined the organization to legitimize their new status through international sporting recognition.

1991 was a banner year for the oval ball, as women's rugby[30] also hosted its first World Cup, bringing together 12 national teams and won by the USA over England[31]. The proliferation of international matches, media coverage and the associated new revenues also confronted the world of rugby with a profound dilemma that would change its history: whether to preserve its amateurism and therefore its traditions, or join the modern era of sport by opting for professionalism.

30. See chapter 47 on women's rugby in the CURRENT ISSUES section
31. The tournament was not approved by the IRFB, but went ahead anyway despite the disapproval of the sport's governing body. It was not officially recognized until 2009

12.

WHY DID 1995 MARK A TURNING POINT FOR SOUTH AFRICA AND FOR RUGBY?

Before tackling the question of professionalism, rugby first and foremost has a date with history. A wind of change swept through South Africa in the early 1990s. The apartheid policy of racial segregation, in place since 1948, had gradually fractured South African society and isolated the country on the international stage.

South Africa's Difficult Return to the International Game After the End of Apartheid

This is also the case on the sporting scene. As illustrated by the Springboks, its national team made up exclusively of white players, which is gradually being sidelined from the world circuit. South Africa and rugby were at the heart of the first mass boycott of a sporting event. In 1976, several African countries boycotted the Montreal Olympic Games because the IOC refused to prohibit New Zealand's participation. The reason: the New Zealand national rugby team toured South Africa that same year, in defiance of UN resolutions calling for a sporting boycott[32].

After this international outcry, sanctions continued to multiply. In the end, it was internal protest and the end of US support with the end of the Cold War that plunged the country and its leaders into a deep crisis. From 1987 onwards, the National Party, the ruling political force of the white minority, had to reform. It began bilateral negotiations with the African National Congress (ANC), the main opposition force long banned from the black population, to put an end to segregation and reintroduce the country to the concert of nations.

It was the presidency of Frederik Willem de Klerk that accelerated these changes. From 1990 onwards, the machinery of apartheid politics began to be dismantled. Political organizations were no longer banned, and Nelson Mandela, the face of the opposition, was released after 27 years in Robben Island prison. The peaceful democratic transition culminated in the first universal elections in April 1994 and Mandela's election as President of the Republic. In his inaugural speech, *Madiba* celebrated the end of apartheid and the birth of a new nation, a *"rainbow nation".*

Yet much remains to be done for a society fractured by over 40 years of racial segregation. Particularly in sport, and especially rugby, which has been one of the main vehicles for this policy. By the end of the 19th century, two rugby federations, one for whites and the other for "coloured players", had already been set up and were already the symbol of chronic segregation. The Springboks team, instrumentalized by Afrikaner power, also embodies this dark legacy.

---

32. See chapter 6 on the genesis of apartheid and the boycott of the 1976 Olympics in the HISTORY section

Organizing a Rugby World Cup is therefore a tremendous opportunity for Mandela. He had the opportunity to open his country's doors to the world once again, to legitimize it in the eyes of other states, and the oval ball, a vestige of apartheid, was the main vehicle for this new chapter in South Africa's history. Thus, during the transition to democracy, de Klerk and Mandela succeeded in convincing the IRFB to organize the 3rd World Cup on their soil.

With the stigma still deep, criticism remains rife. All the more so as Mandela had declared himself a fervent supporter of the Springboks in the run-up to the competition. As a result, the President of South Africa was criticized for focusing more on appeasing the white population than on guaranteeing the rights of black South Africans. Mandela's position was made all the more difficult to defend by the fact that the Springboks team taking part in the World Cup represented the painful weight of the past. All the players are white and come from former Afrikaner strongholds (Western Province, Transvaal, Orange Free State[33]). Chester Williams was the only player of color in the squad, but fate intervened. An injury a few days before the start of the competition forced him to give way to Pieter Hendriks.

The 1995 World Cup: the International Symbol of South Africa's New-Found "Unity"

Nevertheless, the excitement takes over and a certain national reconciliation takes place before the start of the festivities. Springboks manager Morné Du Plessis declares, "*We all have white*

---

33. See chapter 3 of the HISTORY section about South Africa

Why Did 1995 Mark a Turning Point for South Africa and for Rugby?

faces, but our hearts have the colors of the rainbow. It is the people of South Africa who give us our strength and will". Archbishop and anti-apartheid activist Desmond Tutu says: *"Until this year, I couldn't stand the Boks. But now I'm a 100% supporter".*[34] However, the declarations of the main opinion leaders fail to mask the heavy atmosphere within the country, where the shadow of civil war still hangs overhead.

It is against this tense backdrop that the third Rugby World Cup in history is taking place. And it all began with a real-life test for the South Africans, as they faced the reigning world champions, Australia. In front of 45,000 spectators at Cape Town's Newlands Stadium, the Springboks managed to win the game 27-18. Fervor grew in South Africa, especially as the national team easily qualified for the rest of the competition with victories over Romania (21-8) and Canada (20-0). After this match, Hendriks is suspended, allowing Chester Williams to join the squad and add a little more symbolism to a team whose performances go beyond the purely sporting.

A context that is becoming increasingly pressing as the final approaches. Already, the Springboks have eliminated Samoa with a convincing 42-14 win, including four tries from newcomer Chester Williams! The semi-final against France, on the other hand, had all the makings of a real test, but the match was already becoming more than just a sporting affair. Despite South Africa's 19-15 victory in difficult conditions on a pitch soaked by downpours, there were still many suspicions surrounding the South African victory and Derek Bevan's dubious refereeing. As a result, Pierre Berbizier, coach of the French national team, said that he had experienced *"one of*

---

34. Jean-Pierre BODIS, *Le rugby : De l'esprit de clocher à la Coupe du monde*, Éditions Privat, 1999, p.130

the greatest swindles in the history of sport" and that *"the political dimension outweighed the sporting aspect of this World Cup*[35]*".* A view shared by third row Abdelatif Benazzi, who was denied a crucial try late in the match: *"We didn't understand all that [the political context, the end of apartheid] until the final, when we were invited. That was a real eye-opener. It was an extremely powerful moment, and one that went a long way towards easing my disappointment at being denied a try in the semi-final. During the final, I realized that this World Cup was much more than a sporting event. In the end, it's a good thing for this country, and the story is just as good*[36]*."*

The final between New Zealand and South Africa on June 24, 1995 was much more than just rugby. The All Blacks were considered the favorites, having won all their matches, scoring over 40 points including a 145-17 victory over Japan, and included the revelation of the World Cup: a certain Jonah Lomu, who had already scored a record 7 tries in the competition. The final was a breathless affair, with Johannesburg's Ellis Park packed to the rafters with 60,000 spectators. At the end of regulation time (9-9), the two teams were unable to settle the tie, and this World Cup final went into extra time for the first time. It took all the guile of fly-half Joel Stransky to score a drop-goal and allow South Africa to win the long-awaited title.

What happens outside the match will remain even more etched in the history books. Nelson Mandela, wearing a Springboks rugby shirt and cap, handed the trophy to the white South African captain

---

35. *"Berbizier 'swindled' in 1995"*, Rugbyrama.fr, August 29, 2011
36. *Benazzi: "I flattened on the line"*, Interview Rugbyrama.fr, August 9, 2011

François Pienaar in front of a euphoric crowd. Mandela would then have these words. *"Thank you for what you have done for South Africa"*, to which Pienaar replied, *"whatever we have done, no one, Mr. President, will do more for South Africa than you have done for her*[37]*"*. The strong relationship between the two men was illustrated in Clint Eastwood's 2009 film *Invictus*.

But it's hard to measure the significance of South Africa's victory in words. Former Afrikaner leader de Klerk declared that *"Mandela won the hearts of millions of white rugby fans*[38]*"*. However, this symbolic event was not entirely unanimous in terms of national reconciliation. Rugby was seen as the sport of the privileged white class, as opposed to soccer played by the discriminated black majority population.

Although popular enthusiasm was present, it should be noted that, for certain matches, the stadiums could appear to be predominantly attended by white spectators, due in particular to unequal access to sports facilities and tickets. Although initiatives were put in place to encourage a greater mix, many black and colored South Africans were unable to attend matches and show their support for the national team. In *hindsight,* the suspicions of doping surrounding the South African team and a strange case of food poisoning suffered by the All Blacks a few days before the final will also somewhat tarnish this poignant scenario.

In the end, it was the African Cup of Nations, won on home soil in 1996 by the South African soccer team (*Bafana Bafana), which had* a far greater impact at national level. According to Neil Tovey, the white captain of a truly *mixed* victorious team, *"in terms of social*

---

37. Jean-Pierre BODIS, *Le rugby: De l'esprit de clocher à la Coupe du monde,* Éditions Privat, 1999, p.134
38. *"Mandela rallies Springboks",* BBC Sport, Oct. 6, 2003

cohesion, this victory was twenty times more powerful than the Rugby World Cup because it was the sport of the black community, which represents 80% of the population[39]".

Sport thus played a key role in South Africa's long process of national reconciliation. In the words of Nelson Mandela: *"Sport has the power to change the world. It has the power to inspire. It has the power to unite people as few other things can. Sport can create hope where there was only despair. It's more powerful than government in nation building. It's more powerful than racism in building mutual understanding. It's more powerful than apartheid in building reconciliation[40]."* Even if sport, far from being the stuff of fantasy, cannot miraculously solve everything. The 2010 Football World Cup in South Africa will demonstrate that there is still much to be done off the pitch to heal the wounds of past divisions.

1995: The Birth of Professional Rugby

In any case, this World Cup has accelerated rugby's change of dimension, given the international attention generated by the South African context. The 1995 World Cup is now watched in more than a hundred countries, by nearly a billion television viewers. The world of rugby is at a crossroads.

Behind the scenes, the nations of the southern hemisphere (South Africa, New Zealand and Australia) have been hard at work since the early 1990s. Just a few days before the start of the South African World Cup, the three federations have already accepted

---

39. Neil Tovey, *"Sport is far more influential than politics,"* SoFoot.com, Alexander Doskov, February 6, 2017
40. Nelson Mandela at the Laureus Sports Awards ceremony on May 25, 2000

Why Did 1995 Mark a Turning Point for South Africa and for Rugby?

an offer from billionaire media magnate Rupert Murdoch, who is acquiring exclusive rights to broadcast their matches for a decade for $550 million. Meanwhile, a certain Kerry Packer has already contacted the best players in these countries to set up a parallel professional circuit.

Overwhelmed, the IRFB had to react. As Vernon Pugh, one of the body's presidents that year, explained at the time[41]: *"In some countries, rugby is already professional. It's a fact, a reality. It was hiding behind false appearances and that's not good. Then we wanted to avoid at all costs the gulf that was going to widen between North and South, and the Board had to show its ability to accompany the evolution of rugby[42]."*

The IRFB Council (made up of representatives from South Africa, Australia, New Zealand, the 5 Tournament nations and Argentina) met on the night of August 26-27, 1995, and agreed to put an end to amateurism. The IRFB President, Frenchman Bernard Lapasset, decreed rugby *"open"*, the word *"professional"* still being taboo.

The floodgates were clearly open. South Africa, New Zealand and Australia create the SANZAR federation. Its purpose is to manage the Tri-nations competitions and the Super 12, the first annual championship between clubs from the three countries. Rugby's northern hemisphere adapts in the process, but always with a certain nostalgia for the end of amateurism. France and England set up fully-fledged professional leagues in 1995 and 1996, while the first European Club Cup was introduced the same year. Its name,

41. The post then rotates between the representatives of rugby's eight historic nations
42. Jérôme PRÉVOT, *"Un jour, une histoire: 1995, et le rugby changea d'ère"*, Rugbyrama.fr, March 30, 2020

the Heineken Cup, heralded the arrival of sponsors and the marketing aspect that would profoundly transform rugby's traditions.

As for the IRFB, it dropped the word "soccer" from its century-old name and became the International Rugby Board (IRB), thus fully entering this new international chapter of rugby.

13.

HOW HAVE WORLD CUPS ANCHORED CONFRONTATIONS BETWEEN NATIONS IN THE NORTHERN AND SOUTHERN HEMISPHERES?

After 1995, the World Cup became a permanent fixture, thanks to the new media coverage and the sources of funding generated by its broadcasting. The World Cup in South Africa laid the foundations for a competition broadcast in over a hundred countries, attracting hundreds of millions of television viewers. What's more, the following event in 1999 generated commercial revenues of over 200 million euros, half of which came from television rights[43].

As a result, the Rugby World Cups are attracting an ever-growing audience and a growing economy, while at the same time becoming an integral part of the sporting calendar. Since 1987, they have been held without interruption every 4 years, rotating between the northern and southern hemispheres, so characteristic of the forces at work in rugby. In 1987 in New Zealand, in 1991 in the countries

---

43. Jean-Christophe FÉRAUD, *"le ballon ovale gagne du terrain à la télévision"*, LesEchos.fr, October 1st, 1999

of the V Nations Tournament, in 1995 in South Africa, in 1999 in Wales[44], in 2003 in Australia, in 2007 in France, in 2011 in New Zealand, in 2015 in England, before, as we shall see, an unprecedented opening on the Asian continent with Japan in 2019.[45] The choice of an odd-numbered year has been maintained, thus avoiding competition with major international sporting events such as the Olympic Games and the Football World Cup.

In any case, the Rugby World Cup has increased the number of direct confrontations between the nations of the northern and southern hemispheres. This was already the case after the Second World War, with the development of means of transport and communication, but the prospect of a major international tournament has increased the number of test matches. For example, Australia met England just 9 times over the period 1945-1987, compared with 42 times between 1987 and 2022, while New Zealand played France 20 times over the period 1945-1987, compared with 39 times between 1987 and 2022.

Some World Cup matches have anchored this historic opposition between the two hemispheres in popular culture. These include the matches between the XV de France and the All Blacks in the 1987 and 2011 finals, but especially the 1999 semi-final at Twickenham. In that match, Les Bleus overturned a 14-point deficit against New Zealand to claim a splendid 43-31 victory. Or the clashes between England and Australia. Matches between the two teams have often given rise to incredible scenarios. Such was the case in the 2003 final, when Jonny Wilkinson's drop-goal in the last minute of extra time secured the Rose's first and only world title against the Wallabies.

---

44. Initially organized in Wales, several World Cup matches will be held in neighboring Britain and Ireland, as well as in France
45. See chapter 16 on the 2019 World Cup in Japan

The World Cup has also served to rank the powers that be in a truly official tournament. The nations of the southern hemisphere have clearly dominated, winning 8 of the 9 editions: 3 for New Zealand (1987, 2011, 2015), 3 for South Africa (1999, 2007, 2019), and 2 for Australia (1991 and 1999). France, meanwhile, is the nation that has been a finalist in the competition most times without ever winning it (1987, 1999, 2011). The northern hemisphere has only ever won one title, with England in the 2003 World Cup in Australia, and it's now been 20 years since a northern nation last won the World Cup.

However, the gap between rugby's two historic lands has never been narrower: at the dawn of the 2023 World Cup, New Zealand is no longer the world's leading nation, having topped the World Rugby rankings from 2005 to 2019. In 2023, Ireland will occupy 1st place, closely followed by France, while the nations of the southern hemisphere (New Zealand 3rd, South Africa 4th, Australia 7th) have never looked so doubtful with such a low ranking.

14.
WHY ARE SO FEW OF RUGBY'S "NEW NATIONS" MAKING THEIR MARK AT THE WORLD CUP?

In this confrontation between the historic rugby nations of the northern and southern hemispheres, it is clear that few new countries are emerging at the World Cup. However, the tournament has expanded since 1999, from 16 to 20 teams taking part in the final phase. The qualification system has also been widely opened up. 34 teams took part in the 1991 World Cup qualifiers, while those of recent editions (2011, 2015, 2019) have brought together more than 90 countries. A great leap forward at international level, and a testament to the IRFB's evolution.

Rugby's governing body has definitively opened up to the world by changing its name to "World Rugby" in 2014. Today, it brings together 130 national federations. This is less than the number of federations involved in team sports such as soccer (FIFA, 211) or basketball (FIBA, 214). However, the globalization and professionalization of rugby are relatively recent phenomena, with the sport requiring a minimum of tradition and "rugby culture", players and infrastructure.

Despite a more open qualification system, few new countries have ever qualified for the World Cup. Since the inaugural tournament in 1987, with 16 nations invited, only 10 others have managed to qualify at least once for one of the other 9 editions. This pattern is repeated for the 2023 World Cup, where 17 of the 20 qualified teams have played at least 6 times. Chile will be one of the few exceptions with a first appearance, and will therefore be only the 26th country to take part in a Rugby World Cup (compared with 80 for the Football World Cup).

A Closed Qualification System and a Significant Difference in the Level of Play

This may be due to the relatively new nature of the competition, but also to its qualification system. From 1991 onwards, the quarter-finalists of each previous edition qualified automatically for the World Cup. From 2011, this system was extended to the top 3 from each of the 5-team pools from the first round of the previous World Cup. This may act as a brake on the integration of new countries taking part in the World Cup, as only 8 of the 20 places remain to be decided.

In addition, the number of places allocated to the different continents can also be questioned. Europe can have up to 9 representatives, i.e. almost half of the participants. While the low number of places allocated to Asia (1) and Africa (2, including South Africa) is understandable, given the vast differences in the level of the national teams and the lower level of popular interest, it reinforces the presence of the same national teams. World Rugby is currently considering the possibility of increasing the number of teams to 24 for the 2031 Rugby World Cup in the USA.

Nevertheless, it's difficult to challenge this hierarchy and shake up the traditional lines of rugby without a renowned performance. The various slaps in the face received in the past by Namibia (142-0 against Australia in 2003), Uruguay (60-3 against England in 2015) or even more recently by Canada (66-7 against South Africa in 2019) bear witness to the fact that it takes some time for a national team to progress in contact with the best nations. What's more, outside the World Cup, these 2nd and 3rd-ranked teams, still far from being fully-fledged professionals, have few opportunities to play against World Rugby Top 10 teams, and play fewer matches throughout the year. This situation has been exacerbated by the consequences of the Covid-19 pandemic.

The circle of 8 historic rugby teams almost always qualifies beyond the 1st group stage. Only 5 other teams have qualified for the quarter-finals: Fiji (1987, 2007), Samoa (1991, 1995), Canada (1991), Argentina (1999, 2007, 2011, 2015) and Japan (2019). These last two cases are of particular interest to us. They are the most telling evidence that the World Cup can, with rare exceptions, enable "new nations" to join the gotha of world rugby. Even though, as we shall see, the practice of the oval ball has been anchored in these two territories for over a century.

The Rare Case of Argentina and the Emergence of Japan

The first exception is undoubtedly **Argentina**. The country went from emerging nation at the 1987 World Cup to established rugby nation from 2007 onwards. Argentina would later join the exclusive club of Southern Hemisphere rugby in 2012. Argentine rugby is a special case, however, as the oval ball has a long history. It was introduced to the country at the end of the 19th century by a large British community based in Buenos Aires. Its federation, created in 1899, is one of the oldest in the world, and its national team played its first international match on June 12, 1910. After a 1965 tour of South Africa, the Argentine national team made a name for itself on the rugby scene, acquiring the nickname Pumas[46].

Argentina's breakthrough came at the World Cup. Having previously won only once in three appearances, they qualified for the quarter-finals in 1999, with a convincing victory over Ireland. In 2007, Argentina caused a sensation by beating hosts France in their opening match. They went on to lose to South Africa in the semi-finals, but managed to secure 3rd place with another victory over hosts France. Thanks in no small part to this performance, and to its many successful international test matches, Argentina joins the circle of rugby nations in the Southern Hemisphere. In 2012, Argentina joined the Tri-Nations Tournament, which became the Rugby Championship, and once again reached the last four of the 2015 World Cup.

Apart from this case, the other nations emerging at the start of the 21st century did little to confirm their expectations at the Rugby World Cup. **Italy** in particular. The Squadra Azzurra joined the V Nations Tournament in 2000, enabling its national team to regularly compete at the highest European level. Twenty years on, progress has yet to be made. Italy have never won the Tournament, now known as the VI Nations, and regularly come last, with the wooden spoon as their "reward[47]". The same is true of the World Cup, where Italy has never reached the quarter-finals. However, despite their

---

46. See the Argentina chapter in the NATIONS section
47. The name of the virtual "reward" for the team that loses all these matches in a VI Nations Tournament

lack of success against top-ranked teams at the World Cup, the Azzurri XV regularly finish 3rd in the group phase of the first round, easily separating themselves from other more modest teams.

The latest case where the World Cup has allowed a national team to reveal itself is **Japan**. Since the 2010s, the *Brave Blossoms'* level has been rising steadily. Again, a World Cup match in 2015 illustrates this trend: a 34-32 victory over the Springboks in the group phase. Over the course of their international career, Japan have become one of the Top 10 teams in world rugby, showing that they have come a long way from the severe 145-17 defeat they suffered at the hands of New Zealand in 1995. It is this steady progression of the Japanese team, the development of professional rugby on its territory, the renewed popularity of the sport and the prospect of World Rugby extending its frontiers, that will justify the organization of the 2019 World Cup being devolved to Japan for the first time.

15.
WHY IS THE 2019 WORLD CUP BEING HELD FOR THE FIRST TIME IN ASIA, IN JAPAN?

The Rugby World Cup remains a recent international sporting event if we compare it with the first Olympic Games (1896) or the World Football Cup (1930). The seven editions since 1987 have been staged in traditional rugby countries, and it was not until the sport slowly opened up to the rest of the world that other prospects emerged. Japan was one of them, and in 2009, it was the country of the Rising Sun that won the bid to host the 2019 World Cup. A definite opportunity for World Rugby to develop the sport in a new part of the world.

However, the oval ball is far from an unknown land. As mentioned at[48], rugby first arrived in Japan in the mid-19th century, when the first British merchants and academics arrived. The sport was then taken up by the locals, with the first clubs founded in 1890 and a veritable craze developing in the 1920s, with 1,500 clubs and 60,000 members in the archipelago. This was also the period when the first

---

48. See chapter 3 in the HISTORY section

Japanese rugby federation was created in 1926, and the first match of the national team, the *Sakuras*[49], took place in 1932. The team really came into its own in the 1980s, taking part in the first World Cup in 1987, with a historic victory over top-ranked Scotland in 1989.

Yet, despite this long tradition and a clear domination of the Asian scene, Japan remained a "small" rugby nation, regularly swept aside in the most competitive matches. It wasn't until 2003, when Hiroaki Shukuzawa took charge of local rugby, that the first professional championship (Top League) was created, and Japan adopted a genuine sporting strategy for the sport. As a result, the national team progressed and began to make a name for itself on the world stage, while rugby gained in popularity in the archipelago. As a result, Japan is now a serious contender for a World Cup. After failing to secure the 2011 and 2015 editions, Japan managed to convince its peers in 2009 to secure the organization of the 2019 World Cup. A strategic choice for Japan, but also for World Rugby.

On the one hand, for the Japanese authorities. They wanted to develop the practice of the oval ball among the Japanese population, at a time when enthusiasm for the sport, and for the national team, was growing. The organization of such a competition also had another objective: to continue Japan's strategy of staging major international sporting events on its soil, following the success of the Football World Cup in 2002. The aim is to enhance the country's international image and boost tourism. The Rugby World Cup is one of the milestones, as is the bid to host the 2020 Olympic Games later in 2013.

Japan also represents an opportunity for World Rugby. International rugby's governing body wants to turn a new corner

---

49. See the Japan chapter in the NATIONS section

Why is the 2019 World Cup Being Held for the First Time in Asia, in Japan?

in the 2000s and look to other territories, other markets, likely to bring new players, new viewers and new economic prospects. Such was the case on the Asian continent, with its 4.5 billion inhabitants, where only Japan, Hong Kong and a few other countries were "converted" to rugby at the time. World Rugby is therefore capitalizing on this World Cup to open up new avenues and ensure that its major tournament leaves a legacy in Japan and the rest of Asia.

Japan knows, however, that its World Cup can only be a success if its XV team performs well. From 2012 onwards, it was under the guidance of Australian coach Eddie Jones that the national team prepared for the event in the best possible way. The resounding 34-32 victory over South Africa at the 2015 World Cup, dubbed the "Brighton Miracle", confirmed the Japanese XV's clear progress. Although they were subsequently eliminated in the 1st round of the competition, the performance was impressive. It enabled the first Japanese franchise (the Sunwolves) to join the Southern Hemisphere Super Rugby league in 2016[50]. The Japanese league is also in the spotlight, and a number of the sport's stars, such as New Zealander Dan Carter and Australian Matt Giteau, don't hesitate to sign for Japanese clubs. This further legitimizes the fact that Japan is becoming a true land of rugby.

The 2019 World Cup in Japan will be a success on many levels:
- Sporting. The *Brave Blossoms* did better than in 2015, with two victories over major nations Ireland and Scotland. This enabled them to reach the quarter-finals for the first time in their history, although they were subsequently eliminated by eventual winners South Africa.

---

50. International rugby union competition pitting the Australian and New Zealand franchises, and formerly the South African and Argentine franchises, against each other

- Popular. 1.7 million tickets were sold for the 45 matches played. This is the 3rd best total in history, behind the English World Cup in 2015 (2.4 million) and the French World Cup in 2007 (2.1 million). 242,000 international fans from 178 countries came to watch the event in Japan. Stadium capacity reached 99%, although some 1st round matches had to be cancelled due to typhoon Hagibis.
- Media. A total of 857 million viewers watched the competition, which was broadcast in over 200 countries, more than in 2015 in the UK (678 million). Particularly in "emerging markets", where 52% of viewers who watched the global tournament saw matches for the first time. As Bill Beaumont, President of World Rugby, puts it: *"This World Cup in Japan has been the most revolutionary in bringing the game to new audiences and attracting new fans."*
- Economic. The 2019 World Cup generated 360 million euros in revenue for World Rugby, compared with 330 million four years earlier. According to an EY report, the World Cup generated 4.4 billion euros in economic benefits for the country, injecting 2.5 billion euros into Japan's GDP[51].

A new international outlook for rugby…

---

51. All figures taken from World Rugby's 2020 annual report

16.

Why Does the 2031 World Cup in the USA Represent a New Turning Point for Rugby?

After Japan in 2019, the next Rugby World Cups will take place in more traditional lands (2023 in France, 2027 in Australia). A relative break, since World Rugby validated in 2022 that these next World Cups, both men's and women's, will open up to a new continent by awarding them to the United States. This decision may be questionable, given the sport's lesser popularity in North America, as well as the disappointing results of the U.S. national team (18th in the World Rugby rankings and eliminated from qualifying for the 2023 World Cup after losing to Portugal). It makes even more sense in the light of rugby's much-needed globalization strategy.

After Asia, rugby's governing body, World Rugby, is keen to continue the growth of the sport around the world, with a stopover in North America, where the sport is becoming increasingly popular. Rugby has a long history in the United States, having been brought there by British influence in the late 19th century.

The American national team went on to win two Olympic titles in 1920 and 1924[52].

Competing with other team sports, notably American soccer, rugby then fell into disuse, and it wasn't until the early 1970s that a real federation was formed and the national team revived. The U.S. rugby team, the *Eagles*[53], regularly qualified for the Rugby World Cup (8 out of 10 appearances), but with little success and a poor record of 3 wins and 26 losses. The women's team, on the other hand, has enjoyed greater success, winning the World Cup in 1991 and reaching the final of the 1994 and 1998 editions.

Although rugby is still a minor sport in the United States, due to the delay in its professionalization and the weight of other team sports, it remains an area of development for World Rugby, given the large number of licensees (130,000) due in particular to the university system. The United States also introduced a new professional rugby league in 2018, Major League Rugby. By 2023, it will have a dozen teams, and some of the biggest names in rugby have been able to play there, such as Ma'a Nonu, Mathieu Bastareaud and Chris Robshaw. However, television audiences and average stadium attendance (around 5,000) are still a long way from other team sports such as baseball, American soccer, basketball, field hockey and even the recent fervor around *soccer*. The United States hopes that the Rugby World Cup will have a similar effect to that of the Football World Cup it organized in 1994, which made the game more popular throughout the country.

Despite the limitations of rugby in the United States, a number of factors convinced World Rugby that Uncle Sam's homeland was

---

52. See Chapters 4 and 5 of the HISTORY section
53. See the "United States and Canada" chapter in the NATIONS section

Why Does the 2031 World Cup in the USA Represent a New Turning Point for Rugby?

an appropriate venue for the first World Cup on the American continent. In particular, the modern infrastructure, the American-style showmanship and organization of major sporting events, the high TV ratings for the sport, the size of the North American market (380 million people including Canada) and the large number of players (around 130,000) in the emerging rugby territory of the USA.

A competition taken very seriously by the American authorities since Joe Biden, the President of the United States, had personally taken the pen to support this bid in 2022: *"the United States strongly supports efforts to bring the Men's Rugby World Cup 2031 and the Women's Rugby World Cup 2033 tournament to our country and looks forward to working with World Rugby to help deliver the most successful World Cups in history[54]."*

It has to be said that the American powerhouse has a real strategy for organizing major international sporting events in the 2020s, with the 2026 World Cup (co-hosted with Canada and Mexico), and the Los Angeles Olympic Games in 2028. In this way, the United States aims to show the world its ability to organize major global events, and to shine thanks to these high-profile competitions. At the same time, it aims to reaffirm American leadership, which is increasingly challenged on the world stage by the interests of China.

---

54. Statement on USAbid.rugby - October 20, 2021

17.
WHY IS THE 2023 WORLD CUP IN FRANCE MORE THAN JUST A MAJOR INTERNATIONAL SPORTING EVENT?

On November 15, 2017, France was awarded the Rugby World Cup for the 2nd time. This came as a bit of a surprise, as it was South Africa's bid that was favored by World Rugby president Bill Beaumont at the time. Nevertheless, the French bid was able to rely on several factors: its rugby tradition and the country's fervor for the sport, the quality of its infrastructure, thanks to the renovation of the Euro 2016 stadiums in France, and significant financial arguments. In particular, the prospect of "record revenues" for the 2023 World Cup, with a projected 135 million euros in additional revenue compared to the 2015 World Cup, an increase of almost 40%. And therefore a potential increase in the budget of World Rugby, which lives off the economic spin-offs of this major event[55].

---

55. Adrien Pécout, "Mondial 2023: la stratégie gagnante du rugby français", Le-Monde.fr, Nov. 16, 2017

As part of its bid, France pledged to pay 407 million euros to the body, whereas according to a 2017 Deloitte report commissioned by the French Rugby Federation (FFR), revenues from the 2023 World Cup could reach 500 million euros[56].

This victory is part of a policy of organization led by France around major international sporting events at the dawn of the 2010s. This began with Euro 2016, a lever that convinced and reassured World Rugby, and continued with other major competitions such as the Ryder Cup and the Women's World Cup in 2019. Another point of particular interest to World Rugby's governing bodies was the fact that, a few months earlier in 2017, France had been awarded the organization of the 2024 Olympic Games in Paris. And therefore the prospect of extending the fervor around the oval ball with the Olympic Rugby 7s tournament.

In any case, these bid successes have enabled France to lift its head after a series of failures, most notably its duel with London for the 2012 Olympic Games. Lessons were learnt and a new strategy was put in place, particularly in terms of diplomatic lobbying. In this way, France will once again shine thanks to its ability to convince the world to host the biggest sporting events on its territory.

In any case, this Rugby World Cup is generating a lot of budgetary issues, at a time when public funds spent on organizing major sporting events are being called into question. The 2023 World Cup has also been the subject of a number of controversies, including the various trials of former FFR president Bernard Laporte, favoritism surrounding the purchase of tickets, and the ousting of Claude Atcher as president of the organizing committee in November 2022.

---

56. Carole GOMEZ, *"Rugby World Cup 2023: sport at the heart of France's soft power,"* IRIS Institute, Nov. 17, 2017

Since then, the new president, Jacques Rivoal, has been at pains to reassure everyone *that "the World Cup will be profitable. The financial result is secure. Our benchmark is the 2015 World Cup in England, where the context is quite similar"*[57].

As for the overall economic and tourism impact, this is difficult to estimate before the event takes place. In 2017, Deloitte estimated a potential economic impact of around 2.4 billion euros. Although it is always complicated to establish the true repercussions of hosting a major sporting event for the host country, this World Cup will aim to show a flattering face for France during the two months of competition (September 8-October 28). Nearly 2.3 million tickets have been sold, 450,000 foreign tourists are expected and over 800 million TV viewers will watch the competition.

This World Cup also looks to the future, with a certain legacy. The aim is to raise the profile of rugby (through the performances of the French national team), to increase the number of licensed players in clubs (to around 300,000 by 2022) and to create a new buzz around the Top 14 championship.

The other challenge, and it will be a major one, will be to make people forget the chaos of the 2022 Champions League final at the Stade de France and demonstrate that France is capable of organizing a major competition, with large flows of fans and tourists to manage. This makes even more sense less than a year away from the world's biggest sporting event, which will be the Olympic Games in Paris in 2024.

---

57. SudOuest.fr - *"World Cup 2023. Jacques Rivoal: 'We're looking at a profit of 45 to 50 million euros'"* - March 27, 2023

NATIONS
How Was the French National Rugby Team...?

OCEANIA

18.
NEW ZEALAND

From All Blacks to World Domination

We left the New Zealand team in 1905 with a new nickname: the All Blacks. This followed an impressive series of victories on a European tour[58]. This was the first chapter in the long story of New Zealand rugby superiority. A further tour of Europe in 1924-1925 further cemented the New Zealand legend, with 30 victories in 30 matches, earning the team the nickname "The Invincibles". The All Blacks' victorious test-match campaigns around the world and their extraordinary physical and technical abilities made them the most feared team in the world. And the team to beat if you want to claim the title of best rugby nation in the world.

However, from the 1950s onwards, the prestige of the New Zealand national team took a beating. The Springboks' various

---

58. See chapter 3 and the birth of rugby in New Zealand

home tours were controversial, given the apartheid policy and the fact that Maoris were not allowed to travel to South Africa on their first trips. This controversy even led to a boycott by the African nations of the 1976 Olympic Games[59], and also led to strong protests, culminating in the cancellation of such a move in 1986.

Rugby opened up to modernity and international competition in 1987. This did not prevent New Zealand from maintaining its position at the highest level, winning the first World Cup in 1987 and reaching the final in 1995. For rugby fans, these competitions highlight the distinctive style of New Zealand rugby, and for new spectators, the symbols of this New Zealand team, easily identifiable through the players' all-black outfits and the impressive *haka*. The traditional roots of Kiwi rugby thus intersect with the new popular culture of sports consumption, illustrated in particular by the starification of All Black Jonah Lomu after his performances at the 1995 and 1999 World Cups.

The example of Lomu and the new media exposure of rugby's key players help us to understand how New Zealand rugby has been a vehicle for the rehabilitation of Maori culture. New Zealand's population includes 16% Maori, considered the country's indigenous people. Although the Maoris were dispossessed of their land at the end of the 19th century, rugby has gone some way towards preserving their traditions and building a New Zealand national identity between the British colonists and the Maoris. For Matt Te Pou, former coach of the Maori XV team, the reason why Maoris have integrated so well into the national team is that *"their culture is based on the collective, not the individual. Maoris love team sports*

---

59. See chapter 7 on the beginnings of rugby at the Olympic Games

because, for them, the most important thing is the unity of the tribe[60]". Beyond this, the notoriety of the All Blacks and the professionalization of the sport mean that rugby has opened up prospects of social and financial advancement for Maoris, who often come from underprivileged backgrounds. This has even had repercussions beyond New Zealand's borders, as many other Polynesian players in Fiji, Tonga and Samoa see the prospect of playing for the All Blacks as an honor.

The New Zealand team is more than just a sport: it is a true ambassador for its distant homeland, and a unifying force for the New Zealand people. A case in point. Before the 2007 World Cup, each of the 30 players selected received a small capsule containing a piece of the country's soil, from each of the pitches where the 1071 All Blacks have played over the past 102 years. Richie McCaw, captain at the time, is quick to point out that *"our land links all New Zealand cultures together. Whether you're Fijian, Maori, Samoan, Tongan or European, we're all from New Zealand, and the land we stand on is our own[61]".* Rugby is therefore deeply rooted in New Zealand, both in its territory and in its national identity. The country has around 150,000 players for a population of 5 million, and many amateur players in local *Grass Roots Rugby* clubs.

The All Blacks are the most successful national team in rugby history. They have more wins than losses against each of their opponents. Since the creation of the Tri-Nations in 1996, which later became the Rugby Championship, the All Blacks have won 19 titles, making them the most successful team ever. They have also won three World Cups (1987, 2011, 2015). Leading the World Rugby

---

60. "Les Maori, assets des All Blacks", *Le Figaro*, August 31, 2007
61. John NAURIGHT, "Rugby and national identity in New Zealand" [1], Staps, 2007/4 (n° 78), p.101-114

rankings for two decades, the All Blacks will be ranked 3rd in the world in 2023, behind Ireland and France.

Symbols of the New Zealand XV

New Zealand rugby players wear all-black kit. It was Thomas Rangiwahia Ellison, of Maori origin, who proposed the idea in 1893, at the first meeting of the New Zealand rugby federation, as black is a symbol of vitality in Maori culture. It was thanks to this outfit that British journalists dubbed them the **All Blacks in the** early 20th century. Other sources attest that they use this jersey color to mourn their opponents. A white fern adorns their tunic, the other symbol of the country along with the kiwi (bird).

Before each match, the players sing the anthem *God defend New Zealand*, which is available in two versions, English and Maori. The anthem is followed by the **Haka**. This famous dance, first performed by the team in 1905, is a demonstration of pride, strength and unity of a tribe in the Maori tradition. There are several types of *haka*. The best known is **Ka mate**, composed by Maori chief Te Rauparaha in the 19th century. Another, more aggressive version is the **Kapa o Pango**. It was first performed against South Africa in 2005, partly because South African fans had whistled the *ka mate* at a previous match. It is reinterpreted whenever the All Blacks want to show their opponents that they want to fight at all costs. As in the 2011 World Cup final in New Zealand, which they won against France.

19.

AUSTRALIA

Wallabies Revealed through World Cups

Australian rugby's inferiority complex vis-à-vis its neighbor New Zealand at the beginning of the 20th century only lasted for a short time[62]. From 1908 onwards, Australia's XV rugby team enjoyed numerous successes on its European tours, as well as the anecdotal title of Olympic champion in 1908 at the London Olympics. The First World War had a major impact on the development of Australian rugby union. Many of the sport's leaders and driving forces did not survive, bringing competitions to a temporary halt in the two Australian provinces where the sport is most prevalent (New South Wales and Queensland). On the other hand, Australian soccer and rugby union are gaining in popularity.

---

62. See chapter 3 and the birth of rugby in Australia

After 1945, the Australian XV played matches against the world's best nations, but did not enjoy the same success as the New Zealanders. In fact, between 1945 and 1986, the Australians only won 4 of the 23 editions of the Bledisloe Cup (the trophy awarded after matches between New Zealand and Australia). It wasn't until their first world title in 1991, however, that Australia made its mark on the international scene. A few years later, in 1999, they won their second World Cup.

This was a golden period for Australian rugby, with the team regularly winning against rivals New Zealand and becoming the best team in the Southern Hemisphere. Notably after another home final at the 2003 World Cup, but lost to England. Since then, Australia's results have been up and down, despite some solid performances in the Rugby Championship (titles in 2011 and 2015) and World Cups (3rd in 2011, finalist in 2015). On the eve of the 2023 World Cup in France, Australia is only ranked 7th in the World Rugby rankings, well behind New Zealand and South Africa, and has suffered several defeats in 2022 against France, Ireland, Argentina and for the first time against Italy.

Despite the Wallabies' great record of success, rugby union remains in competition with rugby union in Australia. In 2022, 138,000 Australians were registered with rugby union clubs, compared with 175,000 for rugby union and 555,000 for Australian soccer[63]. In addition, the Australian national XIII team, the Kangaroos, truly dominates the international scene, having won 12 of the last 16 World Cups and topping the world rankings.

---

63. Soccer remains the most popular sport, with 1.1 million licence holders - Article Optus Sport, *"crazy' Aussie soccer gap",* Dec. 4, 2022

Australia's XV Symbols

Australian players play in Australia's classic sporting colors, yellow and green, the colors of the golden mimosa, one of the country's symbols. In 1961, the yellow jersey was finally adopted after a tour of South Africa, to avoid confusion with the green Springboks jersey.

The Australian team is nicknamed the **Wallabies** after the wallaby, one of the marsupials found in the country. The nickname has its origins in the Australian team's first tour of Great Britain in 1908. The British media had already come up with a nickname for New Zealand, the famous All Blacks. So they set out to find one for their Oceanian neighbors. At first, they opted for Rabbits, which didn't sit well with the Australian players. For them, the Rabbit is an imported pest. So the whole team decided to take an animal native to their country as their emblem, and to call themselves the Wallabies.

20.
Fɪjɪ

The Origins

Rugby reached Fiji, then a British colony, at the end of the 19th century. The oval ball contributed to the widespread British influence in the archipelago and on the local elites, who spread the practice among the country's various clans. The sport's physical contact and the values it embodied were in keeping with local customs and the ancient avoidance games of the indigenous people, such as *veibona* (a kind of cat-and-mouse game)[64]. A first federation, the Fiji Rugby Union, was created in 1913, enabling rugby to spread throughout the archipelago's 110 inhabited islands. However, due to the country's isolation, it would be some time before a full-fledged national team would compete in international matches.

---

64. Seghir Lazri, *"Aux Fidji, le rugby comme instrument de pouvoir"*, Article Li-bération.fr, Oct. 9, 2019

Fijian rugby first came into its own in 1939, when the Fiji national team became the first team to leave New Zealand without losing a match. This included a stunning victory over the New Zealand Maori team. Following this achievement, a local newspaper writes that *"Fiji are destined to play a major role in world rugby"*. This would prove to be the case, and rugby remains an important element of international exposure for this country, which became independent in 1970.

The National Team

After 1945, Fiji made a name for itself on the international scene after several tours of Australia, New Zealand and Europe. Fiji's first international successes were in rugby 7s, with 5 wins in the first 15 editions of the Hong Kong Sevens[65], putting the small Oceania archipelago on the rugby map. The Fijian XV also performed well, stringing together a series of 15 consecutive victories from 1982 to 1984, and repeatedly winning the Tri-Nations (later the Pacific Nations Cup) despite competition from Samoa.

Invited to the first World Cup in 1987, the Fiji team beat Argentina 28-9 on their debut and then qualified for the quarter-finals, where they were eliminated by the XV de France 16-31. Since then, the Fijian XV has taken part in every World Cup except 1995, and the team's best finish was another quarter-final in 2007. The team is now ranked 13th in the World Rugby rankings.

On the other hand, Fiji has been one of the dominant nations on the rugby 7s scene for several years, with numerous World Sevens

---

65. See chapter 48 in the section Current Challenges for 7-a-side Rugby.

Series victories, three World Cups (1997, 2005, 2022) and, above all, the discipline's first two men's gold medals at the Olympic Games in 2016 and 2021. Quite a feat for a country with a population of 900,000 and around 40,000 players. Although many of them are coveted and join the ranks of national teams and clubs with more attractive economic prospects.

Symbols of the Fiji XV

Fijians traditionally play in a white jersey with black shorts. Their emblem is a palm tree, one of the elements of the Fijian coat of arms and the island's symbolic tree. It also has a strong link with local rugby, as palm wood is sometimes used to build poles and its fruit, the coconut, can be used as a ball for younger players. The XV rugby team is nicknamed the **Flying Fijians** because of the many successes of their 7-a-side team, whose twirling players impress with their speed and power.

The Fiji team performs a war dance, the **Cibi,** before each match. It was during Fiji's 1939 tour of New Zealand that Ratu Sir George Kadavulevu Cakobau, team captain and future Governor General of Fiji, decided that his team should also perform a traditional dance to rival the New Zealand *haka.* So he approached Ratu Bola, the great chief of the warrior clan on the Fijian island of Bau, who taught them this ancestral dance. This new ritual gave the Fijians strength on this tour, as they lost only once in New Zealand. The *cibi has* thus become one of Fiji's distinctive pre-match features.

21.
TONGA

The Origins

Rugby was introduced to the Tonga archipelago after it came under British protectorate in 1900. Rugby was first played in local British schools such as Tupou College and Tonga College. It also spread to the country's royal elites, and was later extended to the 52 inhabited islands of the archipelago. Rugby is a contact sport and, as in Fiji, is in line with the values of Tongan society. The sport grew in popularity over the years, and became a vehicle for consolidating the country's social and political hierarchy around its monarchy, preserved despite the country becoming a British protectorate from 1900 onwards. The country's rugby federation was created in 1923, with the team's first international match against Fiji in 1924.

The National Team

Thanks to the development of communications and transport from 1950 onwards, Tonga was able to break out of its anonymity and make international appearances beyond its neighbors Fiji and Samoa, notably against New Zealand and Australia. It was against the latter in 1973, shortly after Tongan independence had been achieved three years earlier, that the Tongan XV achieved its first major success. Tonga have regularly qualified for the Rugby World Cup (9 times), but have never progressed beyond the group stages. Their most resounding victory was against France (19-14) at the 2011 World Cup in New Zealand.

Like its neighbors Fiji and Samoa, Tonga must regularly field a team from a limited pool of players. This is particularly true of the Tongan archipelago, which has a population of just 100,000 and only 8,000 licensed players. Like its Pacific neighbors, Tongan rugby has to contend with the exodus of many Tongan talents to rugby countries with greater economic prospects, such as Australia, New Zealand and Europe. In some cases, they are even eligible to join other national teams. Tonga was eliminated from the 2019 World Cup in the first round, but 22 of its nationals made up the ranks of the countries qualified for the quarter-finals. This situation has changed since 2020, when World Rugby introduced new rules governing selection criteria for the national team. It now allows players who have not been called up to a national team for 36 months to apply for another jersey. This means that Tonga, as well as neighboring Fiji and Samoa, can pick up some former Wallabies or All Blacks who are no longer called up or who no longer meet the selection criteria because they play in Europe. This should increase the number of Pacific teams and reshuffle the cards in world rugby.

And why not allow Tonga to reach the quarter-finals of a World Cup for the first time. Tonga are the least successful Pacific Island nation (only 3 Pacific Tri-nations titles) and are 15th in the World Rugby rankings.

Tonga's XV Symbols

Tonga play in their country's colors, with a red jersey, white shorts and red socks. Their XV rugby team is nicknamed the **Ikale Tahi** (Sea Eagles), the bird symbol of the island, which is associated with agility and power. Yet it's another bird that adorns their coat of arms, a dove with an olive branch in its beak. This symbol refers to the peace achieved after the civil wars between the 15th and 19th centuries, which led to the unification of the Tongan islands into a single kingdom in 1845.

Like many Pacific rugby nations, Tonga has a pre-match war dance called the **Sipi tau**. The version of the *sipi tau* performed in rugby was written by the former king of Tonga, Tāufaʻāhau Tupou IV, to celebrate a successful tour of New Zealand in 1994. The dance was subsequently performed for the first time at the 1995 World Cup. Although far from being an ancient ritual, *sipi tau* is inspired by Tongan culture and evokes the warrior spirit of their seafaring ancestors. Prior to this, Tongan players performed another traditional dance, known as *kailao*.

22.

SAMOA

The Origins

The last great rugby nation in the Pacific came to rugby later than the others, in the early 1920s with the influence of New Zealand. After the First World War, New Zealand was effectively given a mandate by the League of Nations to govern the day-to-day affairs of the Samoan Islands, which had previously belonged to the German Empire. The Samoan rugby federation was created in 1924, and the first international match was played against neighboring Fiji. Until Samoa's independence in 1962[66], and even afterwards, their rugby remained closely linked to that of New Zealand. In fact, New Zealand did not hesitate to draw on this pool of talent and on

---

66. Western Samoa was so named from 1962, the date of independence, until 1997, when the word "Western" was removed from Samoa.

the Samoan population who had emigrated to its shores to strengthen its team.

The National Team

The Samoan XV has had to wait a little longer than its neighbors
Fiji and Tonga to take on teams from outside Oceania. It wasn't until
the 1980s that the Samoan team began to make other international
appearances, which partly explains why they weren't invited to the
first World Cup in 1987. That didn't stop them from qualifying for
the next one, in 1991, thanks to a XV made up of local players and
Samoans from New Zealand. It was this power-packed style of play
that enabled the Samoans to achieve a real feat: a 16-13 victory over
Wales at their home Arms Park in Cardiff, a historic qualification for
the quarter-finals of a World Cup.

After some fine victories against leading nations in the 1990s
and eleven Pacific Tri-nations, Samoan rugby had to renew itself to
achieve major successes again from the early 2010s onwards (victories against Australia, Scotland and Italy). Samoa's 7-a-side rugby
team also had its moments of glory, with final victory at the 2010
World Rugby Sevens Series. Quite a feat for this small Pacific archipelago of 220,0000 inhabitants, with only around 20,000 licensed
players. The Samoan XV is ranked 12th in the World Rugby rankings.

The Symbols of the Samoan XV

Samoan players wear blue jerseys, white shorts and blue socks,
a reference to the blue of their flag. The jersey features the Samoan

coat of arms. It features the Samoan coat of arms: the sea, a coconut palm, a Christian cross and five silver stars representing the Southern Hemisphere's brightest constellation, the Southern Cross[67].

They are nicknamed the **Manu Samoa, a** reference to an illustrious Samoan warrior. Like other South Pacific rugby nations, they perform a traditional dance before each match, the **Siva tau**. This ancestral, warlike dance is a declaration of superiority. It echoes the struggles of the Samoan people and their culture. It was first performed at the 1991 World Cup.

---

67. This constellation appears on the flag of Samoa as well as on the flags of Australia, New Zealand and Brazil

23.

IN THE REST OF OCEANIA - COOK ISLANDS, PAPUA NEW GUINEA, NIUE...

The Oceania Rugby federation was founded in 2000 and now has 14 members: Australia, Cook Islands, Solomon Islands, Fiji, Nauru, New Caledonia, Niue, New Zealand, Papua New Guinea, Samoa, American Samoa, Tonga, Tuvalu and Vanuatu. Wallis and Futuna, Tahiti and Kiribati are developing federations and are therefore associate members. Most of these nations, with the exception of the 5 mentioned above, do not compete at a high level of rugby, and have few opportunities to play against other teams on a regular basis, mainly due to economic constraints and travel difficulties.

Oceania Rugby organizes the Pacific Nations Cup, which brings together Fiji, Tonga and Samoa. Guest teams such as the New Zealand Maori XV, Canada, the USA, Georgia and Japan also take part. Papua New Guinea also organizes the Oceania Rugby Championship, in which other Oceanic nations compete against each other. Out of 14 editions, Papua New Guinea has won seven, the Cook Islands four, Niue two and Tahiti one.

The Cook Islands, a small autonomous state in New Zealand with just 15,000 inhabitants scattered over 15 islands, are the sixth-ranked nation in Oceania in the World Rugby rankings, with a 53rd place. Papua New Guinea (84th) and Niue (98th) are still a long way behind. However, Niué's performance is particularly noteworthy for a small island of 261 km2 with just 1,900 inhabitants.

AFRICA

24.
SOUTH AFRICA

From Springboks to World Titles

The South African rugby union team was an early factor in the construction of the South African national identity, thanks in particular to the Springboks' many successes over British teams in the early 20th century. Unfortunately, this team reflected the segregationist policies that sidelined mixed-race and black populations in favor of the white British and Afrikaner ruling caste[68].

After 1945, the hardening of these policies, through the implementation of apartheid, meant that South Africa was gradually relegated to the ban of nations. One of its main flag-bearers was the Springboks team, at the time made up entirely of white players and refusing to open up to diversity. South African sport followed the same line, leading to South Africa's exclusion from the Olympic

---

68. See chapter 3 and the birth of rugby in South Africa

movement and to boycotts, such as at the Montreal Olympics in 1976. It was not until the end of the Cold War and the democratic transition brought about by De Klerk and Mandela that South Africa was once again in the spotlight. Mandela did everything in his power to ensure that the 1995 World Cup on home soil was a success, and that the Springboks' first world title marked the reunification of the "rainbow nation[69]".

Back in the international game, the South African team regained its status as a serious competitor to the other great nations of the southern hemisphere. They regularly go toe-to-toe with New Zealand in the Tri-Nations (later Rugby Championship), winning 4 titles in 19 editions. This makes the South African XV one of the most formidable teams on the rugby planet, as they have an overall winning percentage against all other selections, with the exception of the All Blacks. However, when it comes to World Cup titles, South Africa have won as many as their New Zealand rivals, with 3 trophies (1995, 2007, 2019). Current reigning world champions South Africa are not necessarily the favorites for the 2023 edition, as they are ranked 4th in the World Rugby rankings, notably after several defeats to France, Ireland and Australia.

As far as the composition of the South African XV is concerned, the political authorities have been putting mechanisms in place for several years to ensure that the Springboks better reflect the country's multi-ethnic diversity (around 60 million inhabitants, of whom 80% are black, 9% mixed race, 8% white and 3% Indian or Asian). An evolution that takes time, given the weight of segregation policies on South African rugby. As far back as the 1995 title, Chester Williams was the only player of color in the squad. At the

---

69. See chapter 12 on the 1995 World Cup in South Africa

2007 World Cup, there were only 2 mixed-race players in the starting XV, including future star Bryan Habana, and only 6 black and mixed-race players in the entire 30-man squad. As a result, a quota policy was put in place for the 2015 World Cup, requiring that 7 of the 23 Springboks on a team sheet be colored. This has resulted in a team that is more representative of South Africa when it is crowned champions in 2019, including, for the first time in the history of South African rugby, a black captain in the person of Siya Kolisi.

However, for specialist Julien Migozzi, this long transition is due to a number of other factors. In particular, the development of rugby throughout the country, both in towns and villages, access to the best rugby schools for people of color and *"the arrival at the head of the South African federation, national team or clubs, of former players who have played with players of color and whose racism is less exacerbated. They are more likely to inspire confidence in young players and are more aware of their multi-ethnic environment*[70]*"*. South Africa has the second-highest number of rugby club members in the world, after England, with over 650,000 players.

Symbols of the South African XV

South African players traditionally wear green jerseys with gold collars, white shorts and green socks. They have been nicknamed the **Springboks** since the 1906-1907 tour of Great Britain, in reference to the jumping antelope, which has been very present in the country since the 1906-1907 tour of Great Britain. A choice made

---

70. Adrien MAX, *"France - South Africa: "South African rugby accelerates its transition phase" on racial issues",* 20 minutes.fr, Dec. 12, 2022

by the team at the time to prevent the British press from coming up with a nickname for them. The Springbok is thus flocked to the jersey and is the symbol of this team, which will long remain associated with the country's apartheid policy, given its all-white squad for much of the 20th century.

That's why a debate arose around this symbol during the post-apartheid democratic transition in the early 1990s. The new ruling party of the black majority, the African National Congress, wanted to impose the **Protea**, the country's symbolic flower, as the new official emblem of South African rugby. Nevertheless, President Mandela, anxious to preserve a certain national unity, made sure that both the Protea and the Springbok were present on the jersey. The two symbols were intended to materialize his goal of national reconciliation and unity around the "rainbow nation" at the 1995 World Cup on home soil.

The debate continued throughout the 2000s. Finally, it was in 2011 that the first change took place. The World Cup rules were changed, and the World Cup logo was now required on the right-hand side of the jersey. This posed a dilemma for the South African XV, who had previously worn both logos on their jerseys. The authorities decided: the Springbok was moved to the sleeve to make way for the official logos on the front of the jersey. As a result, the Protea is clearly visible on the Springboks' new jersey, and will be in the spotlight when South Africa is crowned champions of the 2019 World Cup.

25.
Namibia

The Origins

The establishment of rugby in Namibia is closely linked to its colonial history. In the 19th century, the first European settlers arrived among the indigenous peoples of this south-west African country, before the territory was officially colonized by the German Empire from 1880 onwards. During the First World War, Namibia was conquered by the Union of South Africa and gradually integrated into this new state, which had a mandate over the country. The practice of the oval ball thus developed in Namibia through contact with its neighbor, with a first federation created in 1916. But Namibian rugby was also strongly affected throughout its history by South Africa's various policies of racial segregation.

The National Team

The first Namibian national team (then known as South West Africa, because it was considered a regional team of South Africa) played its first match against the British Lions in 1955. However, it wasn't until the country's official independence in 1990 that a national team was actually formed. This team took part in the international exposure of the newly independent country, with some astonishing performances. In 1991, for example, the Namibian team won ten matches, including two victories over Italy and two over the great rugby nation of Ireland.

These were probably the only achievements of the Namibian team, whose hopes were not subsequently confirmed. Although they failed to qualify for the 1995 World Cup, they did manage to qualify for the 1999 event, and have been present at every edition since. This brings their total number of appearances to 7 by 2023. Nevertheless, Namibia has never won a World Cup match, and regularly suffers severe defeats, as witnessed by the 0-142 loss to Australia in 2003 and the 9-71 defeat by New Zealand in 2019.

These poor performances on the world stage can be explained by the lack of direct confrontations with the great rugby nations (its first match against South Africa only took place in 2007) and by the poor development of rugby infrastructures. It is indeed complicated to organize regular competitions in this vast country of 2.5 million inhabitants, which has the second lowest population density in the world (3 inhabitants/km2).

Namibian rugby has also undergone a long transitional phase, to enable the majority black African population to take up the sport and ensure that it is no longer just the preserve of the white minority (around 8% of the population). Despite the difficulties, rugby is one of the most popular sports in Namibia, with around 10,000 players. This popularity is due not only to the XV team's presence on the world stage, but also to its dominance on the African continent. Namibia is the most successful team in the Rugby Africa Cup with 9 titles, and won the last edition in 2022 against Zimbabwe. Namibia is Africa's second-best XV rugby nation and is ranked 21st in World Rugby, between Chile and Spain.

The Symbols of the Namibian XV

Namibia's players traditionally wear blue and red shirts and white shorts, reflecting the colors of the Namibian flag. The team emblem is an **African fish eagle**, the country's national bird. They are nicknamed the **Welwitschias**, a plant characteristic of Namibia and very present in its coastal deserts, reputed for its thousand-year longevity in hostile environments.

26.
IN THE REST OF AFRICA - ZIMBABWE, KENYA, ALGERIA...

African national rugby teams are grouped together within the Rugby Africa organization, created in 1986 in Tunis. It has 37 members in 2023 and organizes the Rugby Africa Cup every year. It is structured into several divisions (gold, silver, bronze) to enable different teams to compete at different levels. With South Africa no longer taking part in the competition, Namibia has now won the most trophies (9), followed by Kenya and Morocco (2), and Uganda and Zimbabwe (1).

At the start of the Rugby World Cup era, in the absence of the Springboks, Zimbabwe was Africa's only representative, with appearances in 1987 and 1991[71]. After a brief appearance by Côte d'Ivoire in 1995, it was Namibia who regularly qualified for the Rugby World Cup, confirming their status as the leading African rugby nation

71. The Zimbabwean team was invited over South Africa for this first World Cup, in particular thanks to the performances of its team but also because, since Zimbabwe's independence in 1980, the policy of racial segregation had been abolished in the country, including in its rugby

outside South Africa. It proved this once again during the last qualification campaign, with the Rugby Africa Cup 2022, where it beat Kenya 36-0 in the final.

In fact, Kenya has the second highest number of rugby players in the world, with almost 40,000 licensed players. The country's rugby vitality is growing with the development of 7-a-side rugby, and the Kenyan national team has performed well on the international stage (4th at the 2009 and 2013 World Cups, 3rd at the World Rugby Sevens in 2021).

In XV rugby, African teams, like other second- and third-tier teams in world rugby, have few opportunities to meet Top 10 teams, which limits their development. Behind Namibia (21st), the other countries are far behind with Zimbabwe (31st), Kenya (33rd), Tunisia (38th), Uganda (42nd) and Madagascar (43rd).

Algeria will be one of the African rugby nations to watch in the coming years. Only created in 2015, the Algerian XV put in a great performance at the Rugby Africa Cup 2022, with a narrow semifinal defeat by Kenya (33-36) and a 3rd place finish after a win over Zimbabwe. Algerian rugby is now thinking bigger, with ambitions to take part in real international competitions, like Kenya and Uganda, with the men's and women's Rugby 7s tournaments. And why not dream of the Olympic Games?

AMERICAS

27.

ARGENTINA

The Origins

As mentioned in previous chapters[72], rugby and soccer became an integral part of Argentine society at a very early stage. This was due to British influence at the end of the 19th century, through major investments in public services, trade and transport networks, particularly in Buenos Aires. This explains why Argentina was one of the first territories in South America to set up a rugby federation in 1899 around clubs in the Argentine capital, and to play its first international match in 1910 against the *British Lions*. It was not until the 1950s that the Argentine team really began to make headway. It won the first South American tournament in 1951, after sweeping victories over Uruguay (62-0), Brazil (72-0) and a final win over Chile (13-3). A number of French

---

72. See chapter 4 and the birth of rugby in Argentina

and South African teams were also visiting South America at this time to test their mettle, and the Argentinian XV gradually became a fixture on the world rugby map.

The National Team

The Argentinian rugby team's first trip across the Atlantic took them to Rhodesia and South Africa in 1965. It was during this tour that the team acquired its nickname, the Pumas.

The team gradually integrated itself into world rugby, but it was only after a successful 1999 World Cup that the popularity of rugby in Argentina increased significantly. The Argentine XV went on to win a number of matches against teams from the Six Nations. The 2007 World Cup confirmed this progress, with Argentina going unbeaten in their group, reaching the semi-finals and finishing 3rd in the competition ahead of World Cup hosts France. These consistent performances earned Argentina a place in the 2011 Southern Hemisphere Tri-Nations, which became the Rugby Championship.

Although the Pumas have yet to win this competition, it allows them to regularly face New Zealand, Australia and South Africa, as well as occasionally beating these formidable teams. They defeated New Zealand for the first time in November 2020. Team Argentina continued its progress on the world stage, finishing 4th at the 2015 World Cup. In recent years, however, the team's results have been less convincing, and they are now ranked 8th in the World Rugby rankings. The number of rugby players is rising sharply, with just over 100,000 licensed rugby players, compared with around 900,000 in soccer, for a population of 46 million.

Argentina's XV Symbols

Since 1927, Argentine players have been wearing a light blue and white striped jersey, the colors of the Argentine flag. They have been known as the **Pumas** since 1965. At the time, a South African journalist was trying to find a catchy name for the Argentine team, like the Springboks or the Wallabies. Pumas was chosen, as the journalist mistook the animal on the jersey emblem (a jaguar) for a puma. On April 17, 2023, the Argentine federation decided to permanently transform the visual identity of its crest, replacing the jaguar with a puma.

28.
URUGUAY

The Origins

Rugby first appeared on Uruguayan soil at the end of the 19th century, thanks to the British schools in Montevideo and the Christian Brothers religious community of Irish origin. Despite a long-standing rugby culture, soccer came to dominate, thanks in particular to the first international successes of its soccer team at the Olympic Games (1924, 1928) and the organization of the first World Cup in 1930.

The National Team

Uruguay made its official international debut in 1948, in a match against Chile, then took part in the first editions of the South American Rugby XV Championship, often finishing 3rd, behind rivals Argentina and Chile. In 1960, the Uruguayan team took on one of the Northern Hemisphere's rugby powers, France, for the first time, losing heavily 61-0. Uruguay gradually became the second-largest rugby nation in South America.

The team went from strength to strength, qualifying for its first World Cup in 1999. Since then, they have qualified for the Rugby World Cup 4 times. To date, their record over 20 matches is just 3 wins, against second and third-tier countries (Spain, Georgia, Fiji).

Nevertheless, the difference in level with the leading force in South American rugby, Argentina, is significant. The Uruguayan XV has lost all its official matches against the Argentine XV. On the other hand, they dominate their South American rivals such as Chile, Paraguay and Brazil, ranking 17th in the World Rugby rankings. Uruguay has around 8,000 licensed rugby players (compared with around 400,000 in soccer) out of a population of 3 million.

The Symbols of the Uruguayan XV

Uruguayans play in azure-blue shirts, white shorts and azure-blue socks, recalling the colors of the flag. The Uruguayan rugby team's players are nicknamed **Los Teros**, or the Tero Lapwings, in reference to the country's national bird.

29.
CHILE

The Origins

Rugby was first introduced to Chile in 1894 by British immigrants living in Santiago, Iquique and Valparaíso. Until the 1930s, the game was mainly played by the country's Scottish community. It wasn't until 1953 that the Chilean rugby federation was founded.

The National Team

Chile's first matches against Argentina in 1936 ended in two severe defeats. The team began to compete more regularly in the 1950s. It took part in the first South American championships and was neck-and-neck with Uruguay for second place behind Argentina. They regularly finished 3rd behind Argentina and Uruguay. A member of World Rugby since 1991, Chile has been

evolving since the 2010s, with a first South American championship title in 2015.

It was in 2022, during the World Cup qualifiers, that the Chilean
XV wrote the finest page in its history. The team qualified for its
first-ever Rugby World Cup, following victories over Canada and the
United States. Chile became the 26th country to take part in a World
Cup. The Chilean XV is ranked 22nd in the World Rugby rankings.
Chilean rugby has around 10,000 club-licensed players, for a popu-
lation of 18 million, and is still not nearly as popular as soccer.

Symbols of the Chilean XV

Chile play in red shirts, blue shorts and red and blue socks, recalling the colors of the Chilean flag. The players are nicknamed **Los
Cóndores**, the Condors, in reference to the country's national bird.

30.
IN THE REST OF SOUTH AMERICA - BRAZIL, COLOMBIA, PARAGUAY...

Sudamérica Rugby, created in 1988, is the rugby federation for South America and most of Central America. The confederation currently has 16 members: Argentina, Brazil, Bolivia, Chile, Colombia, Costa Rica, Ecuador, El Salvador, Guatemala, Honduras, Nicaragua, Panama, Paraguay, Peru, Uruguay and Venezuela. It also manages the South American Nations Championship. Argentina is the dominant nation, winning 34 of the 40 editions until 2014, when it withdrew its first team from the competition to concentrate on the Rugby Championship.

The championship is now divided into several divisions. Uruguay has won the 1st division the most times (2014, 2016, 2017 and 2021), ahead of Argentina's reserve team (2020, 2019), Chile (2015), and Brazil (2018). The Brazilian XV is also the 4th-ranked South American nation in the World Rugby rankings (28th), followed by Colombia (37th) and Paraguay (40th), the other emerging rugby nations in the region.

31.
UNITED STATES AND CANADA

Rugby took root relatively early in North America, thanks to British influence. The first clubs appeared in the second half of the 19th century, with a first match in 1874 between university teams from McGill (Canada) and Harvard (USA). However, the sport had a British and therefore colonial connotation, which limited its spread. Rugby also faced difficulties on other fields, with competition from other ball games such as Canadian soccer and American soccer. Oval ball in the United States did, however, see some development at the beginning of the 20th century, due to the fact that American soccer was considered too violent at the time, as demonstrated by the two titles won by the national team at the 1920 and 1924 Olympic Games[73].

The game then collapsed, and it wasn't until the 1970s, with the creation of the Canadian federation in 1974 and the American federation in 1975, that it regained its structure. The development of the game also found a new lease of life in universities, even if it

---

73. See the chapter on the 1924 Olympic Games in the HISTORY section

remained in competition with sports such as field hockey, American soccer, baseball, basketball and *soccer*.

Canada (9) and the USA (8) have taken part in many Rugby World Cups, but only Canadian rugby managed to qualify for the quarter-finals in 1991. Even so, the standard of the USA's **Eagles** and Canada's **Canucks** is in sharp decline, with both teams ranked 18th and 23rd respectively in the World Rugby rankings. They also failed to qualify for the 2023 World Cup.

Ultimately, it's in women's rugby that the two countries stand out. While the American team became world champions in 1991, it's the Canadians who have the best momentum (finalists at the 2014 World Cup and 4th at the last edition in 2021). The Canadian women's XV is ranked 4th in the world, while the Americans are 7th.

Men's rugby in these two countries will undoubtedly experience a new dynamic, as a North American professional league has recently been recreated, Major League Rugby in 2018. The sport continues to grow (135,000 licensed players in the USA, 35,000 in Canada), and rugby is set to enjoy a new lease of life in North America thanks to the Rugby World Cups hosted by the USA in 2031 and 2033[74].

---

74. See chapter 16 on Rugby World Cup 2031 in the USA

32.
IN THE AMERICAS - MEXICO, TRINIDAD AND TOBAGO, JAMAICA...

Rugby Americas North, founded in 2001, is the governing body for rugby in continental North America. It comprises 19 delegations, from the Bahamas to Curacao, Saint Vincent and the Grenadines and Guadeloupe. Its aim is to develop rugby, which is little practiced in the region outside the USA and Canada, the countries with the most players and infrastructure.

Nevertheless, Rugby Americas North has set up competitions, such as the Caribbean Rugby Championship, to develop the level of the other selections. Trinidad and Tobago, Bermuda and Guyana stand out in this respect. In 2023, behind the United States (18th) and Canada (23rd), Mexico (49th), Trinidad and Tobago (50th), the Cayman Islands (54th), Guyana (58th) and Jamaica (66th) can be found in the World Rugby rankings.

Nevertheless, the practice of the oval ball finds more echo through rugby 7s. The RAN Sevens competition allows Jamaican and Mexican selections (see Martinique with a 4th place finish in

2019) to sometimes compete with (encore) selections from Canada and the United States. Jamaica is now a regular guest at the Rugby 7s World Cup.

ASIA

33.

JAPAN

The Origins

After the signing of the Harris Treaty on July 29, 1858, which put an end to more than two centuries of voluntary isolation, rugby was one of the elements that made the opening up of the Japanese Empire to foreign relations a reality. As we have seen, the new British influence led to the creation of the first rugby clubs, notably in Yokohama in 1866 and in Japanese ports[75]. In 1899, at Keiō University, the locals took up the sport and a match was played between two Japanese teams, on the initiative of professors Edward Bramwell Clarke and Ginnosuke Tanaka, both graduates of Cambridge University.

Rugby then experienced a boom at the beginning of the 20th century, a consequence of the strong British presence in the region

---

75. See chapter 4 on Japan in the HISTORY section

with the Anglo-Japanese political alliance from 1902 to 1922. By the 1920s, there were almost 1,500 rugby clubs and over 60,000 players in the archipelago. A first federation was created in 1926, laying the foundations for a national team and a first match in 1932 against Canada.

The National Team

The Japanese XV emerged on the international scene with a victory over the Junior All Blacks in 1968 and a narrow 6-3 defeat by England in 1971. The team went on to become an undisputed force in Asian rugby, winning 11 Asian Championship titles in 15 editions between 1969 and 1996.

A first appearance at the 1987 World Cup and a first victory over the Scottish XV in 1989 helped Japan to make a name for themselves, even if their standards were still far from world-class. It wasn't until the professionalization of the Japanese league in the 2000s that any real impact was seen. From 2010 onwards, Japan showed serious progress, winning the 2011 Pacific Nations Cup against Fiji, Samoa and Tonga. In 2014, Japan won a series of ten consecutive Test matches to move into the world's Top 10.

It was really in 2015 that the Japanese team shook up the rugby hierarchy with a 34-32 World Cup victory over a great rugby nation, South Africa: the "Brighton Miracle". The progression is then constant with several victories at their 2019 World Cup on home soil and a first qualification for the quarter-finals[76]. The competition was a great success, helping to perpetuate the sport of rugby

---

76. See chapter 15 on the 2019 World Cup in Japan

in the country, which now boasts over 120,000 licensed players. The Japan XV is ranked 10th in the World Rugby rankings, ahead of nations such as Fiji, Georgia and Italy.

Symbols of the XV of Japan

Japan traditionally plays with white and red striped jerseys with three **sakuras** (cherry blossoms) in bloom embroidered on the chest. This element is considered Japan's national flower. It's the reason behind the team's various nicknames: the *Sakuras* or **Cherry** Blossoms in English, and more recently the **Brave Blossoms,** to emphasize the valour of the team from the Rising Sun.

34.
HONG KONG AND CHINA

Scottish Influence on Hong Kong 7-a-side Rugby

The presence of rugby in China and Hong Kong bears witness to British history on Chinese soil in the 19th century. Indeed, in 1842, with the Treaty of Nanking between China and the United Kingdom, Hong Kong became a British colony. As we shall see, this explains why rugby was particularly popular in the late 19th century. The first XV rugby tournament was organized in 1910 between teams from the Hong Kong Rugby Club, the Royal Navy and the Army. The first federation was created later, in 1952, on the initiative of a number of Scottish notables living in Hong Kong who played 7-a-side rugby.[77]

Continued British rule in China, the flow of immigrants and capital from Europe, and the establishment of Hong Kong as a major port, enabled the game to flourish, although mainly limited

---

77. To find out more about the genesis of 7-a-side rugby, see chapter 48

to the white British community (with initiatives in Shanghai too). It was in 1976 that Hong Kong entered the world rugby map, when two Scottish businessmen, Ian Gow and Tokkie Smith, decided to promote 7-a-side rugby in Asia. With the support of major sponsors Cathay Pacific and Rothmans International, they created the Hong Kong Rugby Sevens. This enabled the tournament to take on a truly international dimension, welcoming teams from New Zealand, Australia, Tonga and Fiji, as well as 8 Asian national teams. Over the years, the competition has grown to include teams from all over the world, and has become a major milestone in 7-a-side rugby.

This changed in the 1980s, with the gradual disengagement of the British from the region and the handover of Hong Kong to China in 1997. Paradoxically, it was during this period that the first Chinese rugby federation was founded. In 2000, Hong Kong even played the Chinese team for the first time in Shanghai, and against all odds, it was the latter that won 17-15 that day.

China: the Next Great Rugby Nation?

Nevertheless, since the early 2000s, rugby has been developing on Chinese territory, more thanks to its 7-a-side version than its XV version. As in soccer, the Chinese Communist Party is developing a strategy around rugby so that China can also shine in this discipline, particularly since the reintroduction of rugby to the Olympic Games in 2016. Substantial investments in infrastructure and training are being made, but will necessarily take time in a country with no rugby tradition.

This explains why China is still a minor nation in XV rugby (82nd in the World Rugby rankings, while Hong Kong is 24th), but is beginning to emerge in the more accessible discipline of 7-a-side. As a result, Chinese rugby is enjoying considerable vitality, with nearly 120,000 players in the country today. The Chinese women's national team is the first to achieve results, having taken part in the most recent World Cups and the 2021 Olympic Games. Emphasis is also being placed on developing the men's team, with the support of former rugby 7s greats such as England's Dan Norton and Olie Philips. The aim is to be more successful on the Asian stage and to try and make a bigger impact at the Olympics, why not in 2024.

The Hong Kong-China Context Takes to the Rugby Fields

As for the Hong Kong XV rugby team, although it has never taken part in the World Cup, it remains a solid Asian team, winning the last 4 Asian Nations Championships since Japan withdrew from the competition. Their performances are more notable in rugby 7s, with regular appearances at World Cups and domination of the Asia Rugby Sevens Series.

The final of the Incheon tournament in South Korea in 2022 was a reminder of the political context surrounding Hong Kong (the democratic exception and the principle of "one country, two systems" have been challenged by several Chinese laws since 2019, provoking numerous demonstrations). For example, during the match between the Hong Kong and South Korean teams, the militant pro-democracy song *Gloire à Hong Kong* was played instead of the Chinese national anthem, provoking a diplomatic incident[78].

---

78. Anthony BELLANGER, *"Hong Kong: chanter (le mauvais hymne) n'est pas jouer",* France Inter, November 15, 2022

As a result, since the beginning of 2023, the Chinese-influenced Hong Kong Olympic Committee has required all Hong Kong sports associations to use the name "Hong Kong, China", or risk losing their funding. This also applies to national rugby teams. The oval ball and sport are therefore also means used by China to strengthen its hold on Hong Kong, with a view to integrating it fully into its territory.

35.
IN THE REST OF ASIA - SOUTH KOREA, SRI LANKA, MALAYSIA...

The Asian rugby federation, Asia Rugby, was founded in 1968 on the initiative of Hong Kong, Japan and Thailand. Today, it has 35 members. An Asian Nations Championship has been held since 1969. Most of these have been won by Japan (25), although South Korea has taken a few titles (5). Since 2018, the Japanese XV no longer takes part in the competition, and Hong Kong has dominated recent editions, in competition with South Korea. Only Kazakhstan, Thailand and Sri Lanka have contested a final in this competition.

While there are still major differences between Japan (10th) and the other Asian nations in the world rankings (Hong Kong 24th, South Korea 30th, Philippines 41st, Sri Lanka 46th, Malaysia 52nd), it's worth noting a certain craze for the oval ball on the Asian continent, particularly through its 7-a-side version. This is particularly true of Sri Lanka and Malaysia, which have around 90,000 and 60,000 players respectively.

Other countries with a less ancient rugby culture are trying to make a place for themselves through this discipline, as we saw with China. This is also the case in the Persian Gulf, with growing interest from Qatar, Saudi Arabia and above all the United Arab Emirates. It is in this country, in particular, that Asia Rugby is headquartered and chaired by the Emirati Qais Al-Dhalai[79].

79. See chapter 50 on the Gulf States in the Current challenges section

EUROPE

36.
ENGLAND

The Rose XV

The England team took part in the very first international rugby match on March 27, 1871, against Scotland. As the birthplace of rugby, England dominated the first editions of the very first international tournament, the Home Nations Championship. Its stranglehold on the British rugby scene was challenged, however, as the standard of play of its rivals rose, and the English team won only two editions of this annual competition between 1890 and 1910. England remained an important nation on the rugby scene throughout the 20th century, winning the V Nations Tournament and competing against the great nations of the southern hemisphere. England, however, were in doubt at the start of the 1987 World Cup, having won just 29 of their 61 matches during the 1980s, and even "winning" the 1983 tournament with a "wooden spoon" after losing all their matches. The XV de la Rose raised their game with the first World Cups, even reaching the final in 1991, but losing to the Australian Wallabies at Twickenham.

At the start of professional rugby in 1995, the English team returned to the pinnacle of European rugby with several V, then VI, Nations Tournament titles (1991, 1992, 1995, 1996, 2000, 2001). Above all, they are the only European team to have won a Rugby World Cup, in 2003 in Australia, thanks to the talent of striker Jonny Wilkinson. During the period 2000-2003, the England team put the rest of the world to the sword, with 44 wins from 51 matches, topping the world rankings. The following years saw the English XV fall from its pedestal despite some solid performances, twice being World Cup finalists (2007, 2019) and winning four Six Nations Tournaments (2011, 2016, 2017, 2020).

Since then, the level of the English team has regressed to 6th in the World Rugby rankings. Setbacks have included defeats to rivals Scotland and Ireland, and above all their worst home defeat at Twickenham 10-53 to France in the 2023 Tournament. Nonetheless, England remains the world's leading rugby union, with around 2 million players and a network of over 2,000 clubs.

The Symbols

The English play entirely in white, with a red rose at the heart of their jersey. This rose has a special significance, as it gives the team its nickname, **"the XV of the Rose".** Above all, it is a symbol steeped in history. The rose has its origins in the Tudor rose, red with a white heart, which is often associated with England today. It symbolizes the union and marriage between Henry VII (of the House of Lancaster) and Elizabeth (of the House of York) to celebrate the end of England's Civil War of the Two Roses (1455-1487). However, subsequent English monarchs continued to be associated with the red rose because they were descended from the House of Lancaster.

But this story doesn't explain how the red flower ended up on the England team jersey. According to historians, it would appear that Lawrence Sheriff, the founder of Rugby School, received permission from Queen Elizabeth I to use this emblem on his pupils' uniforms in the 19th century[80]. The red rose thus became associated with rugby, and was featured on the jersey of the England team in their first match against Scotland in 1871. The symbol has endured ever since.

---

80. https://www.sportnetwork.net/main/s245/st74325.html

37.
SCOTLAND

Le XV du Chardon

As we have seen, the Scottish team took part in the very first international rugby match against England on March 27, 1871, and was the first team to win such a match. The Scottish team won the most Home Nations Championship tournaments in its early days. From 1886 to 1938, they won 14 tournaments. The situation changed after the Second World War, with Scotland winning just three tournaments (1964, 1984, 1986) before the first World Cup in 1987, and even sharing victory on two occasions.

It was this first World Cup, where they finished as quarter-finalists, that brought Scotland to a golden age, led by a fine generation of players, exemplified by the talent of Gavin Hastings. In 1990, the Thistle team finally won a Grand Slam in the Tournament. The 1991 World Cup could have been even better, but a cruel semi-final defeat by England at their Murrayfield stadium put an end to the

Scots' hopes of a world title. The team then went through a period of decline. They haven't won a Six Nations Tournament since 2000, and have failed to qualify for the last four of a World Cup. Worse still, they were eliminated in the group stages of the first round of the 2019 World Cup.

The Scottish national team is doing better, however, having finished 3rd in the latest 2023 Six Nations Tournament. This puts them ahead of England (6th) and Wales (9th) in the World Rugby rankings, in 5th place. Rugby is one of the most popular sports in Scotland, with around 40,000 licensed players for a population of 5 million.

The Symbols

Thistle

Scottish players traditionally wear navy blue shirts and white shorts, the colors of the Scottish flag. The team is nicknamed the **Thistle XV** in reference to the country's national flower. According to legend, it was the thistle that enabled the kingdom of Scotland to thwart a surprise attack by Vikings from Norway in the 13th century. The Norwegian Vikings wanted to surprise the Scots in the middle of the night. The Vikings removed their shoes to avoid attracting attention and reached the Scottish base. Unfortunately, the darkness prevented them from seeing that they were crossing a field full of thistles. The screams of the unfortunates sounded the alarm, and the Scots repelled the invaders to preserve their independence. The thistle has remained a powerful symbol of Scottish nationalism ever since.

"Flower of Scotland"

Traditionally, *God Save The Queen,* the national anthem of the United Kingdom, was sung before each match of the *Scottish* XV. Scotland has no official anthem, as it is not a state but a constituent nation of the United Kingdom (along with England, Wales and Northern Ireland).

It was in the 1970s that *Flower of Scotland,* a song composed in the mid-1960s by Roy Williamson, began to gain popularity in Scottish stadiums. The lyrics extol the unity of the Scottish nation, its landscapes and its historic struggle against England. In particular, reference is made to the Battle of Bannockburn, where Edward II's English army was crushed by the Scots in 1314[81].

Over the years, the song has become popular in Scotland. It was officially sung by the Thistle XV during a home match against France in the 1990 V Nations Tournament. A few weeks later, the anthem was once again taken up by the entire Murrayfield stadium in Edinburgh, in a 13-7 victory over arch-rivals England. The victory gave Scotland its first Grand Slam title in 65 years. In 1993, *Flower of Scotland* became the official anthem of the Scottish rugby union team.

---

81. Christophe PENOIGNON, *"Rétro : Le jour où... "Flower of Scotland" est devenue l'hymne du XV d'Écosse"*, OuestFrance.fr, March 17, 2020

38.
WALES

Le XV du Poireau

The Welsh team played its first match against England in 1881. After a severe defeat and several setbacks in the Home Nations Championship, the Welsh XV emerged at the beginning of the 20th century with a certain "golden age" and several titles and famous victories against the fearsome New Zealand All Blacks. Welsh rugby went through a difficult period between the two world wars, but enjoyed a second golden period between 1969 and 1980, winning 8 Nations Tournaments. The Welsh XV failed to shine at the first World Cups, even suffering a humiliating home defeat at Cardiff's Arms Park to Samoa in 1991.

It wasn't until the 2010s that Wales returned to regular success in the Tournament, which became the VI Nations, and managed to finish 4th in both the 2011 and 2019 World Cups. Above all, the Welsh XV won 14 consecutive matches between 2018 and

2019, reaching 1st place in the world rankings for the first time in its history.

The Welsh national team is based on four regional teams (Ospreys, Cardiff, Scarlets and Dragons) which today play in the United Rugby Championship, the forerunner of the Celtic league. In view of Wales' weak pool of talent for its XV rugby team, as well as to strengthen the level of these clubs on the European stage, the Welsh Rugby Union has decided, since 2017, that any player with fewer than 60 caps with Wales is obliged to play in one of the four local teams if he wants to continue to be selectable.

A situation that will ultimately backfire on Welsh rugby. It is currently in economic crisis, due to the impact of the Covid-19 pandemic on club finances, which has led to threats of strikes by Welsh XV players in 2023. The international players are under contract with their federation, via the provincial clubs, and several delays in payment have been noted.[82] As a result, on the eve of the 2023 World Cup, several internationals decided to leave the Welsh teams to join other clubs where they would be paid on time, even if it meant giving up their selection in the Welsh XV.

The Welsh team finished 5th in both the 2022 and 2023 Six Nations tournaments, and suffered their first defeat in 2022 against Georgia, ranked 11th in the world. As a result, the Welsh team is at the bottom of the world's Top 10, in 9th place. Rugby is one of the country's most popular sports, and is very much part of the Welsh cultural identity, with almost 75,000 registered players for a population of 3 million.

---

82. FranceInfo.fr, *"Six nations 2023: Pourquoi le pays de Galles est en crise avant de jouer l'Angleterre",* Feb. 21, 2023

The Symbols

Leeks

Welsh players traditionally wear red shirts, white shorts and red socks, the color of the Welsh flag. They are nicknamed the **XV of the Leek**. A reference to a battle won by the then-independent Welsh against the English in the 19th century. Saint David, the country's patron saint, is said to have asked the Welsh soldiers to hang leeks from their helmets to help them find their way around and differentiate themselves from the invaders. The Welsh won the battle, and the leek, a kind of lucky charm, became the symbol of the country. Today, the unflattering name of *XV du Poireau is* sometimes replaced by the more intimidating **Red Devils** or **Dragons**.

The Feathers of the Prince of Wales

Another characteristic symbol of the Welsh team is the coat of arms on their jerseys, which features a **crown topped by three ostrich feathers**. This is the symbol of the Prince of Wales. Its origins date back to a battle won by King Edward III during the Hundred Years' War. He is said to have recovered a helmet adorned with three ostrich feathers, which he then presented to his son, who then ruled the province of Wales. It wasn't until the 17th century that the feather became a symbol of the Prince of Wales, and later of Wales, and was featured on the rugby union jersey from its inception in 1881.

"Land of my fathers"

The Welsh XV abandoned the *God Save The Queen* anthem for the first time in a 1905 match against the All Blacks. After the traditional *haka*, the crowd at Cardiff's Arms Park responded by singing *Hen Wlad Fy Nhadau* ("The land of my ancestors"). Composed in 1856, it's a true declaration of love for Wales. The song reminds the Welsh people that *"valiant warriors gave their blood for freedom"*. It is the main anthem sung before matches, although other Welsh songs are sometimes sung, such as *Calon Lan* and *Lawr ar Lan y Môr*.

39.
IRELAND

The Shamrock XV

In the early days, Irish rugby was organized into two federations: the Irish Football Union, covering the Irish provinces of Leinster, Munster and parts of Ulster, and the Northern Football Union of Ireland, covering the Belfast area. The two federations came together to form a unified team for Ireland's first-ever match against England in 1875. The two Irish "unions" united four years later as the Irish Rugby Football Union (IRFU) in 1879. The XV of the Shamrock became one of the four teams in the Home Nations Championship and won some of the first tournaments.

At the beginning of the 20th century, the political context caught up with the island. Irish republican forces were seeking emancipation from the United Kingdom and full independence for the island. Sport played its part in this struggle, as rugby was perceived as a sport of British influence and domination, in opposition to Gaelic sports. One infamous episode bears witness to the importance of sport in the Irish War of Independence (1919-1921). On Sunday November 21, 1920, fourteen British agents were murdered in Dublin by the IRA (Irish Republican Army). In retaliation, British forces went to Croke Park stadium on the same day, where only Gaelic sports were played, and opened fire on the crowd in the middle of a Gaelic soccer match. The result of this "*Bloody Sunday*": over 30 dead and a hundred injured.[83] It would take some time to heal the wounds. The first rugby match to take place in the stadium was a match in the Six Nations Tournament between Ireland and France (17-20), on February 11, 2007. A few days later, on February 24, 2007, the match was even more historic, as England travelled to Croke Park. In a match fraught with symbolism and high stakes, Ireland came out on top with a clear 43-13 victory.

Following the partition of Ireland into two parts in 1922, with the independent Republic of Ireland on one side and Northern Ireland remaining a nation of the United Kingdom on the other, rugby did not opt for division, as other sports federations did, but rather for union. The Irish Rugby Football Union continues to administer the 32 Irish counties and the island's four tradi-tional provinces: Leinster, Munster, Connacht and Ulster (which includes Northern Ireland)[84]. The Shamrock XV is thus the team for the whole of the island of Ireland, bringing together Irish and Northern Irish players. This is also the case in other sports such as cricket and field field hockey.

---

83. Sylvain GACHE, Richard GUÉRINEAU, *Croke Park, dimanche sanglant à Dublin*, Editions Delcourt, 2020
84. Today, the four provinces make up the four major Irish clubs in the United Rugby Championship and European Cups

The Irish rugby team enjoyed a golden age after the Second World War, winning several V Nations tournaments. However, it wasn't until the 2000s, when Irish rugby was restructured with the introduction of federal contracts for its best players, that Ireland, led by the generation of Brian O'Driscoll, Ronan O'Gara and Rory Best, returned to the forefront of the rugby scene. Notably in 2009, with a first Grand Slam, in the VI format of the Tournament. They went on to win the competition on several occasions (2014, 2015, 2018, 2023), making the Shamrock XV a regular contender for the title.

Ireland have also participated in the World Cup since its inception in 1987, but the team has never progressed beyond the quarter-final stage. However, for the 2023 edition in France, it is the favorite, as it occupies 1st place in the World Rugby rankings. Rugby union is a popular sport, although soccer and Gaelic sports remain at the forefront. There are currently over 100,000 licensed rugby union players on the island of Ireland, for a population of around 7 million.

The Symbols

The Three-Leaf Clover

The Irish play in green jerseys, white shorts and green socks, with a three-leaf clover over the heart, giving the team its nickname of the "**Shamrock XV**". The shamrock refers to the means used by Saint Patrick to explain Catholicism and the Holy Trinity to the Irish, and thus evangelize the island in the 4th century. It later became one of Ireland's national symbols.

The Flag of the Four Irish Provinces

Since the Irish rugby union team represents the whole island, the Irish flag is only flown at matches in Dublin, and only in conjunction with a flag from the IRFU, the Irish Rugby Union. It symbolizes the union of Ireland's four historic provinces, whose coats of arms are featured on the flag (an eagle and sword for Connacht, a gold and silver harp for Leinster, three crowns for Munster, and Burgo's cross and O'Neill's red hand for Ulster). At away matches, only this flag is flown, although at the last three World Cups, the Irish team was preceded at the start of its matches by the tricolor flag of the Republic of Ireland and the Ulster flag.

"Ireland's Call"

For a long time, *Amhrán na bhFiann, the* anthem of the Republic of Ireland, was played when the Shamrock XV played host in Dublin, *God Save the Queen*, the British anthem, was played in Belfast, and no anthem was played when the team played away. This inevitably caused unrest within the team.

In April 1995, a special anthem was created at the request of the Irish rugby association: *Ireland's Call*. Since then, this anthem has been played away from home, while in Dublin two anthems are played: *Ireland's Call* and the Irish anthem. This is not the case in Northern Ireland, where in 2007, during an Ireland-Italy match in Belfast, the Irish FA objected to the organizers' wish to play *God Save the Queen* in addition to *Ireland's Call.*

40.
FRANCE

The French XV

The French team played its first match in 1906 against New Zealand. Numerous encounters with British teams led to their inclusion in the V Nations Tournament in 1910. However, it wasn't until 1954 that the French won the tournament. It was also during this period that France enjoyed its first major successes, notably after a tour of South Africa in 1957. From the 1960s onwards, the XV de France became one of rugby's great national teams, winning 5 tournaments, as well as a first victory on New Zealand soil against the All Blacks in 1979.

The French team went on to impress at the first World Cup in 1987, finishing runners-up to favorites New Zealand. The XV de France went on to suffer a number of disappointments, such as the semi-final loss to South Africa in 1995, which was fraught with symbolism[85]. Or the final loss to Australia in 1999, after having upset the All Blacks in the semi-final in a match of anthology (a historic 33-point comeback to win the match 43-31). With another final defeat to New Zealand in 2011, France remains the team that has played the most World Cup finals without ever winning them.

The rest of the 2010s saw the Coq's selection suffer a series of setbacks, even plummeting to 10th in the world rankings. Since 2019, the XV de France has undergone a definite revival under the leadership of coach Fabien Galthié, and is supported by a new generation of talented players, notably Antoine Dupont and Romain Ntamack. In 2022, France won another Grand Slam after a twelve-year drought.

They also went on an impressive unbeaten run during this period, with 14 consecutive victories, including against Australia and South Africa. Above all, the XV de France inflicted its heaviest defeat on England at Twickenham on the score of 53-10 last February during the 2023 Tournament.

These performances put France in 2nd place in the World Rugby rankings, not far behind Ireland. Rugby is a popular sport in France, driven in particular by its clubs and its Top 14 championship, which remains one of the world's top leagues. Yet rugby remains only the tenth most popular sport in the country, with around 300,000 licensed players, compared with around 2 million for soccer.

---

85. See chapter 12 on the 1995 World Cup in South Africa

The Symbols

The Gallic Cockerel

French players traditionally wear blue shirts, white shorts and red socks, the color of the national flag. Hence the nickname **Les Bleus** or **Les Tricolores**.

They wear the **Gallic cockerel** on their jerseys, the bird that symbolizes France. But this wasn't always the case. In the early days, the XV de France had a red ring and a ring as its coat of arms, the emblem of the major French sports organization of the time, the USFSA.

It wasn't until 1911 that the rooster made its appearance. After France won their first match against Scotland in 1911, team captain Marcel Communeau suggested that the team use the Gallic cockerel. This is a traditional symbol of France, and the animal, considered proud and courageous, can also become aggressive. As a result, the national team's symbol quickly gained in popularity, becoming the star element of the XV de France jersey.

41.
ITALY

The Origins

Rugby became established in Italy at the end of the 19th century thanks to British influence, mainly in the ports, particularly Genoa. The oval ball also had a lasting influence in the north of the country, thanks to close ties with neighboring France. Italian workers returning from France may have been the first to bring the game to the Po Valley, particularly to Treviso and Turin.

Italian rugby then developed in conjunction with Benito Mussolini's Fascist party. The Italian leader sought to forge a "new man" through the practice of virile sports. Rugby played a key role in this, leading to the creation of the first rugby federation and championship in 1928, and the first match of the national team in 1929 against Spain. Nevertheless, the fact that rugby was a British-influenced sport limited the Fascist authorities' investment in the sport. They turned to other sports, such as soccer with the organization of the 1934 World Cup on Italian soil, or even created their own sport with *volata.*

The National Team

In the early days, the Italian XV took part in matches against other European teams who were not present at the V Nations Tournament. Their first match in 1929 ended in defeat against Spain. However, France's exclusion from the Tournament in 1931 led to the creation of a European federation, FIRA, enabling the Italian team to take part in its first official competition[86]. After the Second World War, however, the Italian team remained a second-rate international. From 1965 onwards, they regularly took part in the European Cup of Nations, although they hardly ever won, often finishing in honourable positions alongside the USSR and Romania.

Italy's level of play in the 1980s earned them a place among the 16 teams invited to the 1987 World Cup. Despite the defeats, the Azzuri XV progressed steadily, with a narrow defeat by the All Blacks 21-31 in 1991, and important first victories over Ireland in 1995 and France in 1997. This sporting progress, with a generation led by fly-half Diego Domínguez, enabled Italy to be included in the 2000 Tournament, which became the VI Nations.

Since then, the Squadra Azzurra has done little to shine in this tournament. Despite a few victories, Italy have never won the VI Nations and regularly come last, with the wooden spoon as their "reward[87]". The same is true of the World Cup, where Italy has never

---

86. See chapter 8 in the HISTORY section
87. The name of the virtual "reward" for the team that loses all of these matches in a Six Nations Tournament.

reached the quarter-finals. However, despite their lack of success against top-ranked teams at the World Cup, the Azzuri XV regularly finish 3rd in the group phase of the first round, easily separating themselves from other more modest teams.

With New Zealand and hosts France in their group, the 2023 World Cup promises to be a tough one for the Italian XV. Although the team enjoyed a historic first victory against Australia in November 2022, Italy is no longer in the world's Top 10 and is ranked 14th in World Rugby, between Fiji and Tonga. Rugby remains a minor sport in Italy, with around 70,000 players, a far cry from the 4 million in soccer or the 600,000 in basketball.

The Symbols

Italian players traditionally wear azure blue shirts and white shorts, giving them the nickname **"Azzurri"** or **"Squadra Azzurra"**. The coat of arms on their shirts features the Italian flag with **a laurel wreath**. Popularized by Julius Caesar, the wreath symbolizes the victory and grandeur of the Roman Empire. It was worn by Roman emperors, generals and athletes as a reward for their success. The laurel wreath has been Italy's emblem since the end of the 19th century, and has featured on the jersey of the Italian national team since its first match in 1929.

42.
ROMANIA

The Origins

For once, the origin of rugby in a country is not the result of British influence, but rather that of France. The oval ball was introduced to Romania following the return of students from Paris. They set up several clubs in Bucharest from 1913 onwards. A championship was set up in 1914, and the Romanian team played its first match in 1919 against the American XV. The Romanian team took part in the last Olympic XV rugby tournament, at the Paris Olympics in 1924, but suffered severe defeats at the hands of eventual finalists USA and France. It also took part in the first European Nations Cups between 1934 and 1939.

The National Team

After 1945, the Romanian team remained rather isolated, given the "Iron Curtain" dividing Europe as a result of the East-West divide during the Cold War. However, as in most Soviet bloc countries, sport was soon used as an instrument of power and to promote the totalitarian regime in power.

The sport can rely on a certain tradition, and from 1955 onwards, it was able to play its first series of successful matches in England and Wales. These international outings enabled the Romanian team to gain in strength and credibility. In 1959, in front of a 95,000-strong crowd in Bucharest, they came close to achieving a notable result, with a narrow defeat by the XV de France (15-16). The team went from strength to strength. From 1965 onwards, it won 5 FIRA European Nations Cups and defeated V Nations Tournament teams such as Scotland, Wales and France. These convincing performances earned them an invitation to the first Rugby World Cup in 1987, where they won a match against Zimbabwe.

After the collapse of the USSR and the communist regimes of Eastern Europe in 1989, Romanian rugby, like the country itself, suffered the consequences. Romanian sport was a vector of power, as it was for other Eastern "people's democracies" such as the GDR, and was therefore closely linked to the totalitarian regime of Romanian dictator Ceaușescu. The sport had become the standard-bearer of his regime. Romanian internationals were generally drawn from the two flagship teams, Steaua and Dinamo Bucharest (in fact the army and police clubs), and were professionals before their time. The fall of the regime, and with it the associated funding, plunged Romanian rugby into a deep crisis from which it would struggle to recover.

As a result, the Romanian national team has never looked the same since, and has rarely repeated its exploits. They have often qualified for the World Cup, but they have never won a major tournament, winning just 5 of their 25 matches. Today, however, Romania is one of the top nations in the "second division" of European rugby. However, they have gradually lost this status to Georgia, with their last European Nations Championship title coming in 2007. Romania has a relatively small pool of players, with 10,000 licensed players for a population of 19 million. The Romanian XV is ranked 19th in World Rugby, between the USA and Spain.

The Symbols

Romanian players traditionally wear yellow shirts, blue shorts and red socks, the color of their flag. The Carpathian players are nicknamed the **Stejarii** (The Oaks). This tree is a symbol of strength and pride in Romania, and so an oak leaf is featured on the crest of their jerseys.

43.
GEORGIA

The Origins

We have to go back before rugby's genesis in the 19th century to understand why Georgia has such a special relationship with the sport. During the Middle Ages, Georgians played a traditional sport called *lélo*, a ball game very similar to rugby. British influence in this part of the world was very limited, however, as the territory was part of the Russian Empire, and later the USSR, and so rugby was only able to penetrate this territory at a late stage.

However, from the 1950s onwards, rugby gradually took over from *lélo*. Jacques Haspékian, a former Lyon Olympique Universitaire player, was largely responsible for this. In 1959, he first went to Armenia, the homeland of his ancestors, to popularize rugby. However, the Armenian authorities refused all cooperation. They felt that rugby, a sport with a bourgeois and elitist reputation, could not be played in a country that appreciated the proletariat. In neighboring

Georgia, Haspékian met with much greater success. With the support of the Dinamo Tbilisi omnisport club, he succeeded in establishing rugby, despite the disinterest of the Georgian authorities.

It wasn't until the 1960s that the Soviet authorities decided to develop the sport, in a context where sporting performance was an additional element in the Cold War between the Western and Eastern blocs. In 1964, the Georgian Rugby Union was founded, subordinate to the Soviet Union since Georgia was an integral part of the USSR. After the revival of the Soviet championship in 1966, which had been dormant for almost three decades, Georgian clubs were competitive from the outset.

Given its history and a certain tradition of the game, Georgia has always made up a significant proportion of the players in the Soviet national team, formed in 1974. As a result, the USSR team regularly plays a leading role in the FIRA European Nations Cup, alongside France (bis), Romania and Italy. It could have taken part in the first Rugby World Cup in 1987, but refused to do so, as South Africa was not present and was still a member of the IRFB, the world rugby body. The USSR team gradually disappeared with the collapse of the Soviet bloc in 1989.

The National Team

Georgia became independent on April 9, 1991. The Georgian authorities had not waited for their full autonomy to assert themselves as a nation, as they wanted to be present within the world rugby body, the IRFB, as early as 1990. Georgia finally joined in 1992.

However, it was not easy to get off to a good start against strong opponents. In 1992, the Georgian XV joined the continental federation FIRA (now Rugby Europe), which enabled them to take part in the European Nations Championships, but to start in what was akin to the 3rd division. Gradually, the team climbed the ranks and is now one of the leading nations in the second tier of European rugby. Georgia has won the last ten editions of the European Championship, but is not yet eligible for the VI Nations Tournament.

The Georgian team is making steady progress and has qualified for the 2023 World Cup, its 6th consecutive appearance since 2003. However, they have never reached the quarter-finals. However, the Georgian team has been on a roll in recent months, with a new European Nations Championship title in 2023, its 11th since 2000, and a historic victory over Wales in Cardiff. These results are the fruit of an important structuring of Georgian rugby with the creation of Black Lion, a national franchise-team which brings together all the best players left in the country, and which has won the last two Rugby Europe Super Cups.

The Georgia XV is just outside the world's Top 10, ranked 11th just behind Japan. Rugby is one of the most popular sports and is played by around 15,000 players, many of whom are internationals playing for French clubs, for a population of 4 million.

The Symbols

Georgian players traditionally wear burgundy shirts, white shorts and burgundy socks. The players' nickname is **Lelos**, referring to the local traditional sport similar to rugby. *Lélo* is also the Georgian word for a try. The coat of arms on their jersey features a **Bordjgali**, a Georgian symbol of the seven-winged sun, representing eternity. Another of the national team's nicknames derives from this traditional symbol: the Borjgalosnebi, the "Men of the Sun".

44.
PORTUGAL

The Origins

Rugby began to be played in Portugal in the 20th century, with a first match in 1903 around Lisbon by British and then French teams. However, it took a long time for rugby to take root in this land of soccer, and a national team was only set up in 1935, with a first match and a short-lived 5-6 defeat against Spain. The Portuguese rugby federation was created in 1957.

The National Team

Portugal made its first real international appearances in the early 1960s. They won the second division of the first European Nations Cup FIRA 1965-1966. After a draw with Spain in 1983, Portugal managed a sequence of seven consecutive victories from

1984 to 1985, including wins over Belgium, Denmark, Morocco, Czechoslovakia, Poland and Zimbabwe.

The Portuguese team managed to win a European Nations Championship title in 2003 and qualify for their first World Cup in 2007, following victories over Morocco and Uruguay. The Portuguese XV suffered heavy defeats at the World Cup, including a 13-108 loss to New Zealand, but came close to victory in a 10-14 win over Romania. The Portuguese team was celebrated for its commitment and passion, as it was the only team made up entirely of amateur players to compete in this World Cup.

Since then, Portugal has gone from strength to strength, with many of its players playing in France, from the Top 14 to the Nationale 2. In the second division of European rugby, Portugal is behind Georgia and Romania, and competes with teams such as Spain, Belgium and, in the past, Russia. They qualified for their 2nd World Cup by winning the intercontinental repechage tournament against the USA, Kenya and Hong Kong. Portugal has a limited number of players, around 6,000 licensed, but still ranks 16th in the World Rugby rankings, between Tonga and Uruguay.

The Symbols

Portugal's XV players traditionally wear red shirts, white shorts and red socks. They are nicknamed **Os Lobos**, "The Wolves", in reference to the Iberian wolf found mainly in northern Portugal. The coat of arms represents a rugby ball surmounted by the five shields of the Portuguese coat of arms, the *Cinco Quinas*.

45.
IN THE REST OF EUROPE - SPAIN, GERMANY, SWITZERLAND, UKRAINE...

National rugby teams are grouped together within Rugby Europe, which comprises 47 national federations. Since 2000, this structure has organized the European International Rugby Championship, which is contested in a system of several divisions, depending on the level of the teams. Selections that win this championship have no chance of joining the VI Nations Tournament (England, Scotland, Wales, Ireland, France, Italy), as the two competitions are not connected and organized by the same structure.

The European International Championship has evolved through a number of different formats, although it is most often made up of four or five levels. Today, the championship refers to a set of several divisions made up of national teams who play matches over the course of a season. The first division can thus be likened to a "Tournoi des VI Nations B". So far, Georgia has won the most trophies (11), followed by Romania (3) and Portugal (1). The other regular nations in this second tier of European rugby are Spain (one World Cup appearance), Belgium, Germany and, in the past, Russia[88]. Poland and the Netherlands are the emerging nations now inviting themselves to this stage of the competition.

At other levels, Switzerland won the latest Trophy Challenge (3rd division) with an impressive series of victories, including sweeping wins over Sweden (69-12) and Ukraine (59-32). The Ukrainian XV came second in this division, and the team is looking good despite the fact that the country has been plunged into war since February 2022, following Russia's attack. The Russian XV, like many of its national teams in other international federations, was excluded from Rugby Europe as a result of the Russian-Ukrainian conflict.

Rugby Europe is also setting up a development league to enable certain federations to compete. In 2022, this was the case with Montenegro, Estonia and Slovakia. This was followed in 2023 by the participation of Austria and Kosovo, for whom sporting representation is a means of legitimizing their disputed independence since 2008.

Second- and third-ranked European teams, often made up of amateur players, have few opportunities to compete against the world's Top 10. This competition remains the best way for them to play regularly and progress, as they have little chance of qualifying for the World Cup[89]. In the World Rugby rankings, behind Georgia (11th), Portugal (16th) and Romania (19th) are Spain (20th), the Netherlands (26th), Belgium (29th), Germany (32nd) and Poland (34th). Spain has the most licensed players (25,000), followed by Germany, the Netherlands and Belgium, each with around 10,000.

---

88. Russia has been excluded from Rubgy Europe since the start of the war in Ukraine

89. Apart from Georgia, Romania and Portugal, only Spain (1999) and Russia (2011, 2019) have taken part in the World Cup, without winning a single match

CURRENT ISSUES

46.
How Has Professionalism Transformed Modern Rugby?

In 1995, the traditional sport of rugby entered a new world, with amateurism giving way to professionalism. This brought with it a massive influx of money, via sponsors and television rights, as well as a new craze thanks to its over-mediatization. National professional leagues were formed in both the northern and southern hemispheres, and new competitions emerged. Examples include the Tri-Nations, for which media magnate Rupert Murdoch spent over $550 million to acquire the broadcasting rights for a decade, and the first European Rugby Club Cup, named the Heineken Cup after the tournament's main sponsor. Over the next three decades, the amount of money spent to acquire the rights to broadcast these events, more commonly known as TV rights, continued to rise.

The French Example

The amounts paid for broadcasting the French Championship (Top 14) have risen from 1.2 million euros in 1995 to 113 million euros in 2021. This new and substantial financial windfall is boosting the clubs' structures and financial capacities. Even if, unlike other sports such as soccer, their budgets are still mainly linked to sponsors, although TV rights payments are taking up an ever-increasing share.

The professionalization of rugby and the associated economic stakes have led to an obligation for clubs to achieve results, and the development of a certain arms race. A case in point is Stade Toulousain, whose budget has risen from 700,000 euros in 1998 to 43 million euros in 2019. For the French championship as a whole, a player earned an average of 1,200 euros a month in 1998, compared with 20,000 euros a month in 2019. Since the 2010s, rugby has even experienced a certain *footballization,* with record "transfers" of new rugby stars such as Jonny Wilkinson, Dan Carter and Bryan Habana. However, the biggest salaries in the world of rugby —such as that of Stade Toulousain player and French international Antoine Dupont, who earns 600,000 euros a year, or that of the world's highest-paid player, New Zealander Charles Piutau of English club Bristol Bears, who earns 1.16 million euros a year— are still a far cry from other sports. These include basketball, where NBA player Stephen Curry earns 41.2 million dollars a year, and soccer, with Kylian Mbappé earning almost 72 million euros a year at PSG.

In France, the transformation of rugby into a modern sport has gradually reconfigured the geography of French rugby. Metropolises can more easily mobilize various sponsors to stay in the professional rugby race. Whereas other historic clubs from smaller towns, such as Béziers, Biarritz or Dax, do not have the same ability to attract sponsors to continue their journey at the highest professional level. According to researcher Carole Gomez, French rugby is thus undergoing a form of "metropolization[90]".

The Main Transformations

French rugby is a case in point, but the phenomenon is having repercussions in other countries, leading to more global changes. For example, effective playing time has doubled since the 1990s, rising from 20 to 40 minutes in an 80-minute match. This raises real questions about the physical preparation of players, and the shadow of doping that hangs over this succession of high-intensity matches. Players' health itself is an increasingly recurrent topic, particularly with the growing awareness of injuries and concussions.

A succession of matches with no end in sight, as rugby attracts new players in the sports entertainment sector. As demonstrated by the contract signed in 2021 between the CVC investment fund and the VI Nations Tournament, with a long-term investment of over 400 million euros over five years and a new financial windfall for the six rugby federations. GAFA are also interested in rugby. While Amazon has expressed an interest in broadcasting competitions, Netflix has so far been the first to get involved. A documentary of the 2022 Tournament has been produced, similar to what has been done for Formula 1, tennis and cycling. An opportunity for rugby, weakened by the Covid-19 pandemic, to break out of its straitjacket

---

90. Carole GOMEZ, *Le rugby à la conquête du monde - Histoire et géopolitique de l'ovalie*, Armand Colin, 2019

and develop new sources of economic revenue, explore new markets and attract new fans and future players.

This is already the case with World Rugby's flagship product, the World Cup. It has steadily grown in audience and economic impact. Although this competition is one of the most watched in the world, we have seen that international rugby union has reached a certain glass ceiling. That's why, for some years now, World Rugby has been investing to extend the zone of influence of rugby in two new directions: women's rugby and 7-a-side rugby.

47.
WHY IS WOMEN'S RUGBY THE FUTURE OF OVAL WORLD?

"40,000 spectators will be double the previous attendance record and triple that of any women's event ever held in New Zealand. Millions of people will see the world's best players in action. I hope that many young girls will be inspired to take up rugby. It will be a historic moment and a vibrant testimony to the new dimension of women's rugby. This is currently the main area of progression and development for our sport[91]." This is how Bill Beaumont, President of World Rugby, enthused about the excitement surrounding the latest Women's World Cup 2022, and its final between England and New Zealand at Auckland's Eden Park.

Women's rugby may seem to be the future of the game, but it's by no means a new phenomenon. It developed in the wake of the emergence of rugby in the 19th century, whether in Great Britain, Ireland, France or any other territory that has experienced the

---

91. Interview Vincent BISSONET, *"Beaumont: 'Women's rugby is the main area of development for our sport'"*, Rugbyrama.fr, Oct. 7, 2022

same phenomenon. Nevertheless, there will be many obstacles to women's clubs playing matches on a regular basis. Not least because society at the time was still very patriarchal. Nevertheless, the practice became very popular in the British Isles and France after the First World War, as women replaced men in the popular games of the day, such as soccer and rugby. Little documentation exists on the beginnings of women's rugby, although the work of researchers Anne Saouter and Carole Gomez[92] to put women's rugby into perspective is noteworthy.

It wasn't until the 1960s, with the development of the feminist movement and the fight for numerous rights for women, that women's rugby enjoyed a new lease of life. The road was long and full of obstacles, but this period of liberation gave a new lease of life to the sport, particularly among students. Numerous clubs were founded at universities in Great Britain, Australia and New Zealand, as well as in the USA and Canada.

France was no exception. Women's rugby took shape with the creation of the French Women's Rugby Association (AFRF) in 1970, later officially recognized by the French Rugby Federation in 1989. The internationalization of women's rugby took shape a few years later, with the founding of the Women's International Rugby Board (WIRB) in 1988 and the organization of a World Cup in 1991. At the time, however, women's rugby still faced many obstacles and struggled for recognition. The 1991 World Cup, for example, was not officially recognized by the rugby authorities until 2009.

The professionalization of the sport from 1995 onwards has led to increasing support for women's rugby, which has also managed

---

92. Anne SAOUTER, *Être Rugby: Jeux du masculin et du féminin,* Petite bibliothèque Payot, 2013; Carole GOMEZ, *Le rugby à la conquête du monde - Histoire et géopolitique de l'ovalie,* Armand Colin, 2019

to establish its own regular competitions. Widespread acceptance of the game led to the creation of women's versions of other major XV rugby tournaments, such as the V Nations Tournament in 1999, and the development of its own competitions, such as the Canada Cup and the Churchill Cup. As the years 2000 and 2010 progressed, women's rugby began to make a name for itself, particularly in terms of their style of play, which returned to the early days of avoidance rugby, rather than the increasingly impact-oriented style of their male counterparts. A further step was taken in 2021 when World Rugby officially removed gender designations from the title of the Women's World Cup. As a result, all future World Cups, whether men's or women's, are now called *Rugby World Cups*, with one designation per year.

World Rugby is stepping up its policy of promoting and developing women's rugby. It is following the lead of the major international sports organizations to be a driving force for change in terms of gender equality and inclusion. Female rugby players are also a tremendous asset for world rugby, as in 2018, according to World Rugby, out of 9.8 million players worldwide, 2.7 million are women. That's 30% of all rugby players worldwide. This growth is set to continue, with the governing body estimating that by 2026 this number will have risen to around 40%.

The success of the most recent Rugby World Cup 2022 in New Zealand is no exception. Although postponed from 2021 to 2022 due to the Covid-19 pandemic, it proved to be a brilliant showcase for women's international rugby. In the stadiums of this rugby homeland, attendances were substantial, particularly for the final between New Zealand and England, mentioned at the start of the chapter, with a new record of 42,000 spectators. This was also reflected in terms of television viewership, as the World Cup was broadcast in over 40 countries. In particular, the BBC recorded higher figures than for the previous edition in 2017, with a cumulative audience of over 18 million viewers.

To build on this momentum, in 2023 World Rugby launched a program to step up the development of women's rugby in the run-up to the Rugby World Cup 2025 in England. This includes the launch of a new competition in October 2023, the WXV. It brings together 18 teams, divided into three categories according to their level, to increase the number of international matches and develop the level of women's world rugby as a whole[93].

Nevertheless, the women's teams suffer from the same limitations as their male counterparts. Of the 12 nations that have qualified for the 2022 World Cup, with the exception of the USA and Canada, women's XV teams are limited to the historic rugby nations of the Northern Hemisphere, Southern Hemisphere, Pacific Islands and Japan. New Zealand has won six World Cups, England two and the USA just one. In this respect, the recent introduction of 7-a-side rugby into the Olympic fold since 2016 has breathed new life into the discipline's men's and women's selections, as well as opening up new international prospects. With the Los Angeles Olympics in 2028 and the Rugby World Cups in 2031 and 2033 in the United States, North America is a key target.

---

93. World Rugby website, *"World Rugby launches accelerate to fast track the development of womens rugby"*, April 25, 2023

48

HOW IS 7-A-SIDE RUGBY CONTRIBUTING TO A NEW GLOBAL AND OLYMPIC HORIZON FOR OVAL WORLD?

"When I arrived at the head of World Rugby (in 2007), we were coming off the back of a great World Cup in France, which had broken all records for stadium admissions, audience figures and merchandising. But I felt the need to set rugby within a larger international frame of reference. Because in the end, in a World Cup, you always find the same nations. I said to myself: 'If we don't get out of this environment in which we pamper ourselves, we're going to get bored.' Rugby risked becoming sclerotic. So what could be done to increase the number of members? How could women's participation be developed? The right tool was rugby 7s. It was already well established among British players, and was the ideal format for taking rugby to the big leagues: the Olympics! With 7-a-side, I could bring rugby into the wider world[94]". So it was that Frenchman Bernard

---

94. Interview with Clément DOSSIN, *"Bernard Lapasset: 'Jonah (Lomu), you don't impose on him what he's going to say'"*, lequipe.fr, August 6, 2016

Lapasset, Chairman Emeritus of World Rugby, came up with the idea of reintroducing 7-a-side rugby to the Olympic Games.

Indeed, rugby union remains a sport that has difficulty breaking through certain boundaries to achieve true globalization. There are a number of obstacles to overcome, such as the specificity of the rules and player profiles, the number of protagonists on the field, the need for infrastructure and a certain rugby tradition and culture in the territories where it is to develop. Rugby 7-a-side, with a reduced number of players and a format of two 10-minute halves that allows several matches to be played in a day, thus remains a new alternative. It could enable rugby to penetrate new territories, increase the number of players and attract new television viewers. In short, to compensate for the imperfect globalization of XV rugby, with its premier discipline, XV. This explains the motivation behind World Rugby's efforts to convince the Olympic movement. The result was a vote in 2009, at the 121st Olympic Congress in Copenhagen, to reintroduce rugby to the Olympic Games, after its exclusion in 1924[95].

1883: Birth of 7-a-side Rugby

However, the discipline is not something that has been constructed from scratch in order to re-enter the Olympic fold. Rugby 7s has a long history, having been invented in 1883 by Ned Haig and David Sanderson, two butchers from the small Scottish town of Melrose. Their club was in financial difficulties, prompting the two friends to organize a rugby tournament to raise funds, with teams of 7 players and reduced playing time to increase the

---

95. See the chapter on the 1924 Olympic Games in the HISTORY section

number of matches and the spectacle. Thanks to the success of these matches, 7-a-side rugby became popular in Scotland, and then in other rugby lands throughout the 20th century.

It was much later, in 1973, that the 7s reached a turning point. The Scottish Federation organized the first international tournament in Edinburgh, featuring 8 teams. Given the popular success of the event, two Scottish businessmen wanted to develop such a competition outside Europe with the support of sponsors. The Asian market attracted their interest, due to the vitality of the Hong Kong rugby federation, with its *Scottish* influences.[96] The first edition was organized in 1976 with 12 national teams, including New Zealand and Australia. The tournament became firmly rooted in time, bringing together different national teams outside the traditional framework of rugby. This enabled other selections, such as Fiji and Samoa, to emerge victorious from certain tournaments.

The World Sevens Series Revolution

This openness to the world was clearly reflected in the first Rugby 7s World Cup, held in Scotland in 1993. 24 nations took part, compared with 16 for the 1991 Rugby XVs World Cup. The Netherlands, Taiwan and Latvia, for example, were a long way from the traditional home of rugby. The 1998 Commonwealth Games, held in Malaysia, were the first major international multisport event to include the sport. In 1999, 7-a-side rugby embarked on a tour of the continents with the launch of the World Rugby Sevens Series, a series of international tournaments across the globe. The

---

96. See the Hong Kong and China chapter in the NATIONS section

first edition was held in countries where there had been no official international rugby competitions before, such as Tokyo in Japan, Punta del Este in Uruguay and Dubai in the United Arab Emirates.

Among the first national teams to take part in the Sevens were, once again, countries not usually represented at major international Oval events, such as Morocco, Russia and Papua New Guinea. Since then, the World Series Sevens have been held every season, with stops all over the world, including England, France, Australia, the USA, Hong Kong, Singapore and Dubai. Although New Zealand remains the dominant nation with 14 titles from 24 editions, nations such as Fiji (4 titles), Samoa (1 title), and even Kenya (3rd in 2021), stand out. This diversity is somewhat less evident in the women's event, dominated by Australia and New Zealand, but which regularly includes new selections such as China and Colombia. In this way, 7-a-side rugby is opening up new horizons for the world of rugby, successfully establishing itself in the four corners of the globe and promoting new national teams among the 130 member federations of World Rugby.

The International Craze for World Cups and the Prestige of the Olympic Games

The **Rugby 7s World Cups** are part of this opening-up. 40 different nations have participated at least once in one of the 8 editions, compared with 26 countries over 10 editions for the XV. Argentina, Hong Kong, Russia and the United Arab Emirates have already hosted the competition. The format is also developing at women's level, who have been competing in the same events as the men since the 2009 edition, with 24 different nations having taken part at least once in one of the last 4 World Cups. On the men's scene, New Zealand, England and Australia stand out, but teams such as Samoa, Kenya and Fiji (3 titles) compete with these great rugby nations.

The Fiji team has been the Olympic revelation since the reintroduction of **7-a-side rugby to the Olympics** in 2016. The men's editions saw the Fijian team, a historic rugby nation of just 1 million inhabitants, crowned in 2016 and 2021. For the women's editions, Australia (2016) and New Zealand (2021) won the gold medal[97]. This gives rugby new exposure, as the Olympic Games are one of the most watched sporting events in the world, with around 3.5 billion viewers.

In fact, this new Olympic perspective could have jeopardized the 7-a-side World Cup, since World Rugby had proposed, in 2013, that this competition be discontinued in order to guarantee the Olympic event the greatest prestige. However, the decision will not be taken, as the World Cup allows for the inclusion of more nations (24) and it is possible to adjust the dates of the event to accommodate a smaller Olympic tournament (from 12 to 16 teams).

It's true that these World Cups are competitions that extend rugby's international leverage, both in terms of the nations present and the number of bids to host the competition. For the last edition in 2022, which took place in South Africa, no fewer than 12 countries bid to host the event, including Germany, India, Tunisia, Jamaica and Qatar. All the more reason to push back rugby's frontiers a little further.

-----

97. It's worth noting the special case of the teams from Great Britain during this Olympic tournament. Wales, Scotland and England are represented at the Olympic Games under a single banner, that of the British National Olympic Committee. This is not the case in rugby, as it is in soccer, since the 3 nations have their own federations, historically very old, which are members of World Rugby

49.
WHY SHOULD SOUTH AFRICA JOIN RUGBY'S NORTHERN HEMISPHERE AND THE SIX NATIONS TOURNAMENT?

The geography of rugby has historically been divided between two parts of the world, the northern and southern hemispheres. This can be explained by the role of European tours in the 20th century of the so-called "southern" nations (South Africa, Australia, New Zealand and later Argentina, Fiji, Samoa and Tonga), who came to compete with, and sometimes dominate, the self-proclaimed more powerful European nations.

The professionalization and commercialization of rugby from 1995 onwards has not swept away this observation. The proliferation of test matches and World Cups has even materialized and reinforced this rivalry between the two hemispheres[98]. The growing interest of broadcasters and sponsors has even enabled the southern hemisphere to set up genuine competitions, as in Europe, notably in 1995 with the Tri-nations for national teams and the Super Rugby league for clubs.

---

98. See chapter 13 of the WORLD CUP section

The latter originally brought together teams (franchises) from South Africa, New Zealand and Australia. As of 2016, an Argentinian team has even been included, as well as a Japanese team a few years later.

However, Super Rugby is a complex multinational competition between widely separated territories. As a result, it has gone through several format changes over the three decades of its existence, in search of the ideal model. This has made the competition even more fragile, as it is costly to organize, tiring for the players and difficult for the public to follow.

South Africa's Exclusion from Super Rugby, the Southern Hemisphere Club League

In 2020, Covid-19 hastened the downfall of Super Rugby. Due to pandemic-related travel restrictions, the competition was unable to resume in its original format. This prompted rugby federations in Australia and New Zealand to launch their own tournaments. Faced with the continuing economic difficulties of Super Rugby and the new sporting appeal of these national competitions, the two federations proposed a hard-hitting reform of Super Rugby at the end of 2020. It no longer included teams from Argentina and South Africa, in favor of teams representing the Pacific islands, thus making it a competition on a more regional scale. As Mark Robinson, Chief Executive of the New Zealand Rugby Federation, explained at the time, *"We want teams to be competitive, and for fans to want to see them play each other every week*[99]*".*

---

99. Dépêche AFP, *"Un Super Rugby sans l'Argentine ni l'Afrique du Sud: Le projet explosif des Néo-Zélandais"*, July 17, 2020

This decision precipitated the divorce with South Africa. Their four teams (Bulls, Lions, Sharks and Stormers) withdrew from the Super Rugby structure to focus on European competitions. Julie Roux, CEO of the South African federation, is quick to point out that they *"are delighted at the prospect of a closer alignment and the search for a future in the northern hemisphere. However, we would not have taken this decision without the actions from elsewhere [Australia and New Zealand]"*.

While this decision may come as a surprise, both geographically and ecologically, it is a little less so if we look at the economics of rugby and the consumption of matches, and therefore at the issues of broadcasting, TV rights and time zones. For example, the biggest difference for South Africa with Great Britain and Ireland is 2 hours for six months each year, compared with 11 hours with New Zealand. This is an advantage for South African viewers and interests, as it aligns them more closely with Europe.

South Africa's Gradual Integration into European Leagues and European Cups

From the 2021-2022 season, the South African franchises will join the URC (United Rugby Championship). This is the championship of the Scottish, Irish, Welsh and Italian provinces. Two South African franchises reached the final of the competition that season, with the Stormers claiming victory. In the 2022-2023 season, the performances of these South African teams enabled them to enter the European Cups for the 1st time, through the Champions Cup and the Challenge Cup.

These new moves are not only controversial from an ecological point of view, but also reflect the isolation of South African rugby.

As Yann Roubert, the French clubs' representative on the EPCR board[100] explains, *"the carbon footprint is obviously a black mark on this integration, but the South African provinces are bound to have a very negative footprint, because the country is isolated. This is one of rugby's great misfortunes. As long as we want France-South Africa, we'll have to travel halfway around the world, but we know that's far from ideal".* These problems were already present in the old Super Rugby version, when the Argentinian and South African teams had to travel to Oceania. This is set to accelerate, given the issues surrounding global warming, the growing media coverage of rugby and the interest of certain countries, such as Qatar, in staging high-profile matches.

South Africa's Inclusion in the Six Nations Tournament Is not yet on the Agenda

In the Southern Hemisphere, a return of South African teams seems increasingly unlikely. Super Rugby season 202 sees the entry of new regional franchises. The first is Moana Pasifika, affiliated to the New Zealand federation, which aims to represent the Pacific nations, particularly Samoa and Tonga. The second is the Fijian Drua franchise, which previously competed in the Australian national championship. On December 2, 2022, New Zealand Rugby and Rugby Australia definitively adopted this competition system until 2030, renaming the championship Super Rugby Pacific. The door is now closed for South African rugby.

---

100. European Professional Club Rugby is the governing body and organizer of two interclub rugby competitions: the Champions Cup and the Challenge Cup.

Could South Africa's new integration into the northern hemisphere mean a changeover for its national team? Will the Springboks leave the Rugby Championship for the Six Nations Tournament? While this could be an attractive proposition for tournament organizers, in terms of the South African market, nothing has been decided yet.

As Benjamin Morel, Managing Director of Six Nations Rugby Limited [the entity that organizes the Tournament] explains, *"there is no current plan to extend the Tournament to other nations. We're really happy with the current competition and focused on preserving the Tournament as it is. On the other hand, we're concentrating our efforts on the July and November windows to create competitive series between North and South. This is the future, because it could enable emerging nations to join the elite, without necessarily having to go through the Six Nations*[101]*"*. Since 2020, Six Nations Rugby Limited has been organizing a competition between teams from the two hemispheres, called the Autumn Nations Series. The Autumn Nations Series replaces the traditional touring and test matches, with the aim of increasing the revenue associated with these high-stakes fixtures. This new competition is a further step towards anchoring rugby a little more firmly in the sporting industry, with the declared aim of increasing the number of matches between the major teams. The aim is to increase the number of matches between the big teams, and thus expand the audience for rugby, making it an increasingly lucrative, globalized sport.

---

101. Interview Arnaud Coudry, *"Six Nations: le patron du Tournoi dément l'intégration prochaine de l'Afrique du Sud dans la compétition"*, lefigaro.fr, January 24, 2023

50

UNITED ARAB EMIRATES, QATAR, SAUDI ARABIA... WHY ARE THESE PERSIAN GULF COUNTRIES NOW INVESTING IN RUGBY?

The modern evolution of rugby, notably through women's rugby and rugby 7s, has enabled certain countries to join the world of rugby and become part of a new international media and sports scene. However, modern sport is not only about the performance of athletes and teams, but also about the spectacle associated with the event. At the end of the 1990s, many investments in sport came from states with no real sporting tradition, seeking to capitalize on the beneficial effects of organizing such competitions.

Qatar's Pioneering and Successful Sports-Political Strategy

This is particularly true of **Qatar**. This small Persian Gulf country, barely larger than Corsica and with a population of around 2 million, has been investing in sport since 1995. Its main objective at the time was to emancipate itself from the influence of its neighbor, the great regional power Saudi Arabia. The Qatari emirate relied on sport, and its so-called "positive" and "universal" values, to make a name for itself on the international scene and set itself apart. This was particularly true of its neighbors, who were renowned in other fields: oil for Saudi Arabia, finance for Bahrain, commerce for Dubai (the most glitzy emirate in the United Arab Emirates at the time).

This strategy paid off, as Qatar, thanks to the financial strength of its gas resources, was able to sponsor and organize competitions on its soil throughout the 2000s. These included the ATP tournament in Doha, the Qatar Motorcycle Grand Prix and the Asian Games in 2006. The culmination of this strategy came in 2010, when Qatar won the bid to host the 2022 World Cup from the United States. Qatar then stepped up its investments, whether through PSG or the international media network BeIN Sports. It has also organized numerous world championships (athletics, cycling, handball) on its territory.

The United Arab Emirates and its Stranglehold on Asian Rugby

As if by mimicry, other Persian Gulf states were quick to follow suit in this quest for exposure and sporting prestige. They see it as a means of international exposure that can act as a gas pedal to prepare their economic systems for the post-oil era. Bahrain and, above all, the **United Arab Emirates** are a case in point. This federation of emirates is also banking on sport to shine on the international stage, improve its image and support its economic diversification plan. It was one of the first Persian Gulf countries to invest in rugby. The country is particularly renowned for its 7-a-side rugby, influenced by the British heritage that is still very much alive in the country after it gained independence in 1971.

A heritage that is very much alive in the most prestigious emirate, **Dubai**, through several tournaments, and which became one of the first destinations outside the traditional field of rugby to join, along with Hong Kong, the World Rugby Sevens Series calendar in 1999. Since then, the Dubai tournament has become a regular feature of this annual competition, attracting some 80,000 spectators each year and is the first major rugby tournament in the Middle East. For Raphaël Le Magoariec, a specialist in Gulf companies, this event is a real "decompression bubble" for the Western expatriate populations there, and an additional element in the seductive, entertainment-oriented image that Dubai is seeking to build for itself[102].

The event is also part of the global communications strategy developed by the United Arab Emirates and Dubai. Largely financed by Emirates Airlines, the event is part of a drive to promote the country's "brand", while at the same time contributing to Dubai's strategy of being seen as a true "global entertainment city". The tournament is proof that even without the presence of a major local team or a certain sporting legitimacy, the country can shine thanks to the organization of a world-class sporting event. For example, it was Dubai that hosted the final qualifying round for the Rugby World Cup 2023, with a repechage tournament between the USA, Hong Kong, Kenya and Portugal. And yet the United Arab Emirates (ranked 60th in the World Rugby rankings) are a long way from qualifying for such a competition.

---

102. Raphaël Le Magoariec, *"Dubai and sport, image of a fractured society"*, EchoGéo, Dec. 31, 2021

And yet, the Gulf States remain committed to developing rugby in their respective territories, and thus to embodying the sport itself. In 1993, the Gulf Cooperation Council (GCC), made up of Bahrain, Kuwait, Oman, Qatar, Saudi Arabia and the United Arab Emirates, launched a project to create a rugby union team representing all these countries. On July 3, 1993, the **Persian Gulf team** played its first match, losing 20-64 to Namibia. Between 1993 and 2010, the Persian Gulf team took part in several international matches. Although they didn't achieve any major successes, they did lay the foundations for the construction of a rugby league of their own in the region and in Asia, outside the South-East Asian area.

For the time being, only one team from the Gulf regularly takes part in the Asia Rugby Sevens Series: the United Arab Emirates. In fact, the team put in an interesting first performance, finishing 3rd in the 2022 edition, behind favourites South Korea and Hong Kong. The UAE's influence on Asian rugby is significant, as the governing body for rugby in Asia, Rugby Asia, is based in Dubai, and its president is none other than Qais Al-Dhalai from the Emirates.

Saudi Arabia, the New Sports Banker in a Hurry

The growing interests of the United Arab Emirates and Qatar are arousing the covetousness of the Gulf's rival and regional powerhouse, **Saudi Arabia**. The petro-monarchy is one of the last countries in the region to have invested heavily in sport, making it an important lever for accelerating its global transformation plan, Vision 2030. Spearheaded by the country's leader, Crown Prince Mohamed Ben Salmane, Saudi investment in sport has intensified since 2018, with new high-profile offensives since 2021 and the end of the blockade vis-à-vis Qatar. This is illustrated by the takeover of Premier League club Newcastle, the transfer of soccer stars such as Cristiano Ronaldo and Karim Benzema to the Saudi league at a premium price, and the takeover of the global golf circuit by Yasir al-Rumayyan, the head of the Public Investment Fund (PIF). This Saudi sovereign wealth fund, estimated to be worth $600 billion, steers the financing of political and sporting investments and is behind such pharaonic projects as the "city of the future" Neom.

Sportwashing and the Testing of Sport's "Neutrality" in the Face of its So-called "Positive" Values

These state-supervised financing schemes are coming in for increasing criticism. In particular, they are accused of **sportwashing**: using the positive virtues conveyed by sport to improve a country's image, while masking its shortcomings in terms of respect for human rights or the environment. These issues are very present in Western societies today, even if these criticisms have little effect on the economics of the sports industry itself. The example of the 2022 World Cup in Qatar shows that boycott postures have found little echo worldwide. The competition was a media success, with the France-Argentina final watched by 1.5 billion viewers worldwide. In the space of just one month, the Qatari emirate took center stage on the world stage, ignoring criticism of the organization of the tournament and the issue of migrant workers.

Moreover, behind the rhetoric of **"apolitical" and neutral sport**, the various major international sports federations are currently focusing on the economic aspect of organizing their competitions. With the obvious prospect of opening up their sport to new countries that have not yet organized major events. And to penetrate new territorial and fan markets. For the time being, however, little emphasis is being placed on creating real safeguards, specifications and support policies to develop a sport, during the competition period, that is genuinely more ethical, more inclusive and more in tune with the challenges of global warming.

The same applies to rugby. In the future, we can expect to see matches and competitions taking place in these various states, which have stepped up their sporting investments since the success of the 2022 World Cup, a competition that put the entire Persian Gulf region in the spotlight. Qatar, for example, has already bid to host the 2025 Rugby World Cup, following France's withdrawal. The small emirate is also in talks to host European Rugby Cup matches in its brand-new stadiums.

Like the Formula 1 Grand Prix in Bahrain, the United Arab Emirates, Qatar and Saudi Arabia, these Gulf countries, with their different strategies, are acting with a certain mimicry. Qatar's consecration of the soccer World Cup will accelerate the hosting of major international sporting competitions in the region. The growing popularity of rugby, whether for the XV, XIII, 7-a-side or women, could be the new playground for these new state-sports strategies.

Even more so today, sport is a means of power for states, and a way of presenting themselves to the world in a different light, as the USA, the USSR, Germany, France, South Africa, China and Russia have all done. These Persian Gulf states have understood this very well, and have chosen to rely heavily on this lever to build their future and prepare for the post-oil era. Sport will therefore be eminently political for the rest of the 21st century. And even one of the most traditional sports, rugby, cannot escape this.

Acknowledgements

A third book in three years on the world of sport and geopolitics... I wouldn't have believed it just a few years ago. This time, I've left the round ball behind for the oval ball, and thus recalled the fond memories of rugby, for which I first felt a thrill at the frustrating 1999 World Cup. Happily, new memories are being created with the remarkable performances of the French national team and my beloved club, Stade Rochelais.

Once again, this latest book would never have seen the light of day if it hadn't been for the fierce passion for sport that I've shared with my brother Anthony ever since I was a child. A real gateway to my future interest in geography, history and politics. Many thanks to him.

Thanks to my other half, my wife Zoé, who has supported me throughout this third project with her advice, her joie de vivre and, perhaps most importantly, her love.

Thanks to my mother, Nadège, who has always supported me whatever my ideas, projects and obstacles.

Thank you to Jean-Charles Gérard, my publisher, for trusting me once again.

Thanks to my family, to all my friends and family. In particular to the *Relecture club*: Brigitte, Florian, François, Geoffrey, Guillaume M., Guillaume C., Jean-Luc, Mathieu, Romain, Sarah and Vincent.

Thanks to the people who took the time to answer my many questions to make this book as accurate as possible: Arnaud Coudry, Aymeric Milan, Carole Gomez, Hinato d'Asie Rugby, Joseph Ruiz, Pascal Boniface, Pierre Rondeau, Raphaël Le Magoariec, Simon Chadwick, Théo Reunbot alias "Rivenzi" and Thibaut Martinez-Delcayrou.

Thank you to the 70,000 subscribers of FC Geopolitics, the media outlet I founded in November 2019, without whom this new literary adventure would not have been possible.

Finally, a thought for my energetic grandmother Pierrette, and also for my grandfather Aurélio, who left too soon, who always hold a special place in my heart.

Bibliography

Lukas AUBIN, Jean-Baptiste GUEGAN - *Atlas géopolitique du sport,* Éditions Autrement, 2022

Jean-Pierre AUGUSTIN - "Le rugby: une culture monde territorialisée", *Outre-Terre* n°8, 2004

Jean-Pierre BODIS - *Histoire mondiale du rugby,* Éditions Privat, 1987

Jean-Pierre BODIS - *Le rugby: De l'esprit de clocher à la Coupe du monde,* Éditions Privat, 1999

Jean-Pierre BODIS - *Le rugby d'Irlande. Identités et territorialités,* Bordeaux, MSHA, 1994

Pascal BONIFACE - *Géopolitique du sport,* 2nd edition, Armand Colin, 2021

Pascal BONIFACE - *JO Politiques,* Eyrolles, 2016

Jean FABRE - "Football et rugby, ce jeux qui viennent du nord", *Pouvoir,* n°121, 2007

Simon CHADWICK, Paul WIDDOP, Michael GOLDMAN - *The Geopolitical Economy of Sport,* Routledge, 2023

Sylvain GACHE, Richard GUERINEAU - *Croke Park, dimanche sanglant à Dublin,* Éditions Delcourt, 2020

Henri GARCIA - *La fabuleuse Histoire du rugby*, Éditions de la Martinière, 2013

Carole GOMEZ - *Le rugby à la conquête du monde - Histoire et géopolitique de l'ovalie*, Armand Colin, 2019

Guillaume HERBERT - *Rugby en chœurs, Des hymnes et des hommes: voyage en pays d'Ovalie*, Éditions Amphora, 2022

Jean LACOUTURE - *Voyou et gentlemen: une histoire du rugby*, Gallimard, 1993

Denis LALANNE - *Nous reviendrons à Eden Park: le fabuleux roman de la Coupe du monde de rugby 1987*, Éditions Calmann-Lévy, 1987

Raphaël LE MAGOARIEC - "Dubaï et le sport, image d'une société fracturée", *EchoGéo*, Dec. 2021

Thibaut MARTINEZ-DELCAYROU - *Faute ! Dans les coulisses des plus grandes polémiques arbitrales*, Hugo Sport, 2022

Julien MIGOZZI - "Le rugby en Afrique du Sud face au défi de transformation: jeu de pouvoir, outil de développement et force symbolique", *Les Cahiers d'Outre-Mer - Revue de géographie de Bordeaux*, April 1, 2010

Anne SAOUTER, *Être Rugby: Jeux du masculin et du féminin*, Petite bibliothèque Payot, 2013

SO PRESS - *Tampon! La folle histoire du rugby*, Éditions Marabout, 2019

Table of Contents

Table of Contents

Best sellers Max Milo Editions

Hitler's banker, Jean-François Bouchard

Confessions of a forger, Éric Piedoie Le Tiec

The Koran and the flesh, Ludovic-Mohamed Zahed

Governing by fake news, Jacques Baud

Governing by chaos, Collectif

A political history of food, Paul Ariès

Mad in U.S.A.: The ravages of the "American model",
Michel Desmurget

Mondial soccer club geopolitics, Kévin Veyssière

Putin: Game master?, Jacques Braud

Treatise on the three impostors: Moses, Jesus, Muhammad,
The Spirit of Spinoza

TV Lobotomy, Michel Desmurget